Turning Wool into a Cottage Industry

Paula Simmons

A Storey Publishing Book

Storey Communications, Inc.
Schoolhouse Road
Pownal, Vermont 05261

*The mission of Storey Communications is to serve our customers
by publishing practical information that encourages personal independence
in harmony with the environment.*

Cover, text design, and production by Cindy McFarland

Edited by Gwen W. Steege

Cover photos by Nicholas Whitman

Indexed by Joyce Goldenstern

Illustrations on pages 32, 40, and 145 redrawn by Cindy McFarland

Copyright © 1991 by Storey Communications, Inc.

Originally published in 1985 by Madrona Publishers, Inc., Seattle, WA

Printed in the United States by Book Press
Second Printing, September 1995

LIBRARY OF CONGRESS CATALOGING-IN-PUBLICATION DATA

Simmons, Paula.
    Turning wool into a cottage industry / Paula Simmons. — Updated & rev. ed.
       p.   cm.
    "A Storey Publishing Book."
    Includes bibliographical references and index.
    ISBN 0-88266-685-1 (pbk.)
    1. Wool industry—Management.   2. New business enterprises—Management.
    3. Cottage industries—Management. I. Title.
  HD9890.5.S56   1991
  677'.31'068—dc20   91-50000
                                            CIP

Turning Wool into a Cottage Industry
is dedicated to
my dear friend Sachiye Jones,
founder and editor of
The Black Sheep Newsletter
for many years.

Contents

1 • Wool as a Cottage Industry 1

2 • Sheep Breeds and Crossbreeds 5

3 • Sheep Management 23

4 • Selling Wool without Shepherding.........................47

5 • Preparing and Selling Raw Wool............................56

6 • Preparing and Selling Washed Wool......................70

7 • Carding As a Cottage Industry 86

8 • Income-Producing Angles 103

9 • Business and Merchandising Tips 120

10 • Equipment..135

11 • Successful Entrepreneurs 152

Questions and Answers.............................165

Glossary 174

Sources 180

Index 185

Wool as a Cottage Industry

THE VALUE OF WOOL, which is relatively low in the shearing shed, increases quite significantly in proportion to the labor expended upon it during processing. As a raw material, wool offers great possibilities to the entrepreneur. The fleece, straight off the sheep, is not particularly attractive, but it is a versatile material that can be washed, sorted, picked, carded, dyed, and spun into irresistible yarn for the fiber artist, carded into soft warm batts for the quilter, or heated, moistened, rubbed, and shaped into the delights produced by the feltmaker.

More Income for the Sheepraiser

The sheepraiser who wants to develop a cottage industry to realize a better return per pound for wool will need to grow a long-staple wool that is desired by spinners. The farmer has many initial advantages in creating a wool business: A barn or shed can be converted into a wool-processing area and store, and there are sheep on the property to add interest and attract customers. Although the farmer will have a basic knowledge of sheep, wool-shearing, and sorting, expertise must be developed in the areas of processing and marketing to compete with the kind of wool that is now being imported from Aus-

This is where a wool-based cottage industry really begins.

tralia and New Zealand for use by craftsmen. This and other subjects, such as the health of the sheep, their diet and housing, and the cleanliness of wool, are discussed in the next two chapters.

Wool Processing without Sheep

The entrepreneur who wishes to establish a cottage industry based on the purchase of wool for processing and resale also requires a knowledge of sheep breeds, wool selection, and the types and quality of wool most desired by spinners. All this information, and much more, is contained in this book, which is based on my personal experience and that of many others who make a living from wool.

In labor-intensive crafts such as spinning and weaving, the cost for materials is relatively low compared to the investment in labor. Therefore, to attract regular customers who will buy your wool year after year, it is most important to buy and sell only the highest-quality fibers. The benefit to a spinner in buying directly from a dealer or wool processor is the higher quality and greater selection than may be offered when getting raw fleece from a wool grower. Also, when buying processed wool, the user can better evaluate the suitability of the fiber for the end use.

Special Characteristics of Wool

Enthusiasm for the unique properties of wool will help you to handle it with more pleasure and present it for sale with confidence. Wool's remarkable qualities cannot be duplicated — it is a natural and renewable resource. It is strong, warm, resilient, soft, and weatherproof. When converted into clothing, it breathes to allow air to get to the skin, yet it protects, better than any synthetic material, against both extreme heat and cold. Wool can absorb moisture without losing its ability to keep the wearer warm — it actually becomes 5 degrees warmer when it is wet. Hikers and skiers know that wearing wool is their best protection against hypothermia.

Flash-flaming never occurs with wool, making it a safe fiber for all kinds of articles, especially children's clothing, household furnishings, airplane carpets, and upholstery. The Canadian Forestry Service, Western Region, specifies only wool undergarments for fire fighters. Although synthetic fibers themselves may not burn, they do conduct heat, so a wearer's body may be burned.

Sheep: Nonwasteful Consumers

It is not possible to overemphasize the importance of sheep to the world. Over 75 percent of the land on the earth's surface cannot be used for anything but sheep. Sheep do not compete with the production of vegetables, fruit, or cereal grains. These crops require arable soil while a herd of sheep can live on grasslands or rangelands that cannot produce anything except the wild grass. Sheep also fertilize the soil that feeds them. Some vegetarians claim that sheep eat the grains that could be used by humans. This is not necessarily so, for a large part of man's food crops such as corn, rice, and wheat have by-products that cannot be consumed by humans because they are too high in materials such as cellulose for the human system to digest. Sheep, being ruminants with four stomachs, can consume these by-products and thrive on them. In fact, research by the University of Wisconsin states that only 11 percent of the world's land is capable of producing the kind of foodstuffs that can be directly used by humans. Sheep can thrive on much of that neglected marginal land.

The Return to Cottage Industry

Throughout the ages and around the world, the crafts of spinning and weaving have been most respected professions, often enlisting whole families in the various processes from raw wool to finished fabric. After the Industrial Revolution, the drift was away from the land and all its bounties to the acceptance of machine-made products. Happily, there is now again a strong emphasis on back-to-the-land: basic values and real fibers. People are weary of plastic and polyester and the pollutants associated with them, and are looking enthusiastically toward natural materials, organically grown crops, and handmade garments. Again it is considered honorable and most acceptable to be self-sufficient, and the family enterprise has returned, almost in spite of television and other mass-media attractions. A cottage industry can be the key to the good life — enjoyment of healthy living and simple pleasures while working at a profitable home business. Yes, you can make a living from wool. The following chapters will show you various possibilities. One of my previous books, *Raising Sheep the Modern Way*, published by Garden Way, covered the successful raising and care of sheep. This book, which deals with the processing and marketing of sheep-related crops, was written in response to many inquiries about the use of the Cottage Industry carder and because of the interest shown by sheepraisers and spinners during my Wool in Your Wallet Workshop at the black-sheep farm of Sachiye Jones in Oregon.

Sheep Breeds and Crossbreeds

ANY DISCUSSION of sheepraising usually begins with the subject of sheep breeds, whether for purchasing new sheep or working with an existing flock. The selection of the "right" breed will seem momentous to a person contemplating the purchase of the first sheep. The decision can be made easier by balancing breed knowledge against sound practical advice.

Desirable Characteristics

The special breed that sounds ideal may not be available in your area, and when you add up all the costs of transportation, it might be well to reconsider the advantages claimed by this breed and see if they can be approximated closer at hand. A careful breeding program can upgrade the more available breeds and may give many of the desired qualities.

Initially, find out what breeds are being raised successfully by other sheepraisers in your vicinity. These breeds could be well suited to the prevailing climate and type of forage, and a good choice for breeding stock. No matter what sheep you start with, you can go in the direction you want by being selective and keeping only the very best of your lambs for replacements. Just by keeping your best lamb each year and culling out the least satisfactory ewe, you can change a small flock quite substantially in a few years. After you are actually raising sheep, your ideas about breeds may change, and later on you may consider it fortunate that you were unable to get the breed you originally wanted.

There are several advantages in raising your own breeding stock rather than buying more ewes. You can monitor the lamb's growth and control its feed to be sure of good nutrition and fast maturity. You will also know the history of its health and if it has had any difficulties that it seemingly outgrew but still retains genetically. Equally important, you will be taking no chances on buying disease. Once you have a healthy little flock, you must be very careful about the sheep you bring home. This does not mean that you never, ever buy any more sheep; it just means that you should be cautious about buying — buy only when necessary (or irresistible). If you are sure you need longer wool or coarser wool or finer wool, or sure you need larger and faster-growing animals, the easiest way to go in that direction would be the purchase of one sheep — a ram to breed with the ewes you have. He might need to be purebred, but not necessarily registered. Look for good health, good conformation, virility, hardiness, fast growth, and the type of wool that you prefer or that your customers require. There is a lot to be said for the hybrid vigor resulting from a good cross of breeds, as you will see in the following section.

Watch out for untrimmed hoofs, malformed or soft hoofs, or limping sheep. Aside from indicating neglect, these make it more difficult to determine whether the feet are sound or unsound, and bad feet can be an incurable problem. Check for worn-down teeth, runny noses, hard udders (which are evidence of past mastitis), ticks, and poor jaw conformation, such as underbite or overbite (which can affect the eating habits and life span of a sheep as well as be hereditary).

Be a little dubious about buying or keeping for breeding a bottle lamb that was disowned by its mother, since it too may be deficient in maternal instinct. The runt, the one that would have died without your constant help, is also not the one to keep for breeding. You want to perpetuate the strongest animal, the best animal, with all the right instincts.

Choosing a ewe lamb that was one of twins can give the advantage of inherited twinning, which is especially profitable if you have a ready market for locker lambs (meat lambs). Single births are not completely undesirable, for there are circumstances when one large lamb is better than twins growing slowly on a ewe with insufficient milk. You can supplement the mother's milk, but this is a poor substitute for the ewe's own milk. The profit on one lamb may be equal to the profit on two if you have to buy milk replacer and extra grain to feed them.

Another factor to consider is whether the fleece will be long enough to be spinnable when a lamb is market size. On locker lambs, a fleece long enough to sell for spinning could make quite a difference in profits. Lambs, although small, can be difficult to shear, so when there is no real incentive to make shearing worthwhile, the tendency is not to bother. With dark sheep, the main reason for shearing the lambs is that the fleece will never be blacker than it is for that first shearing.

In breeding for wool length or luster or softness, you will not necessarily get the desired features in all of your lambs, so be determined to keep only the best, the ones with the characteristics you have decided are needed.

The University of Wyoming states that "Most traits contributing to wool production are relatively *highly heritable*, and thus will easily respond to selection." Having secured the breed of your choice, with the kind of fleece you want, continue to be selective in your choice of the lambs to keep. Even in purebred flocks, not all individual lambs are equal in wool quality or conformation.

Top profits come from a high weight of salable fleece and from maximum numbers of marketable lambs for the number of ewes, against the cost of feed. The wool should be coming from both the ewes *and* their lambs, which necessitates a fairly long-wool lamb. The number and salability of the lambs will depend on quite a few things: the maturity rate of the lambs, the ewes' fertility (in and out of season), their mothering

Maternal instinct is an important aspect in crossbreeding.

ability, milk production, and prolificacy (ability to produce multiple births). For productivity, the right feed must be provided for both the ewes and their lambs.

When it comes to mothering, certain sheep and certain breeds seem to be better mothers than others. However, mothering can still be influenced by externals: the palatability of the pasture, an undisturbed situation during and right after lambing, and the age and condition of the ewe. The older ewes, especially if well fed, are usually excellent mothers. When buying sheep on a tight budget, an older ewe (from a healthy flock) could be a bargain if she has a sound udder and fairly good teeth.

Heterosis

Heterosis is the hybrid vigor, the increase in performance, that is often found in a crossbreed when it is compared to the average of its purebred parents. The crossing of breeds to get hybrid vigor is the result of selecting a ram with specific advantages, usually large size, fast growth, and hardiness, to crossbreed with ewes that have specific traits of fertility, pro-lificacy, good milk production and mothering ability, plus good wool type and weight. One of the advantages of a cross-breeding program, in contrast to purebreeding and selecting the best for replacement stock, is that crossbreeding can bring out traits that are ordinarily less likely to be in inherited, such as birth weight and, particularly, survival rate. In crossbreed-ing, the progeny from a combination of breeds will have very different characteristics if the breed of the ram is reversed with that of the ewe.

With your resulting lambs, selection strategy must be based on exact information, which will necessitate record-keeping. There are standard recording practices that should include, for each lamb: birth weight, type of birth, weaning weight, 90-day weight, 180-day weight (if the lamb is kept that long), fleece weight at first shearing, age at breeding, and lambing records. If you have a choice of more apparently suitable ewe lambs than you want to keep, you could put them in with the ram at seven months of age and consider keeping the ones that conceive, especially any that have twins. Many breeding authorities consider that ewes who lamb as yearlings are ex-hibiting a trait that promises a profitable life span of lambing. This is not good practice, however, unless the lambs have shown a good growth rate and are in excellent condition.

If you are getting good results from a particular cross-breeding program, then you would do well to continue it, keeping with the original type of cross and retaining some of the best lambs to see how they compare in performance to your original ewes.

Scientific research has concentrated mostly on raising sheep for qualities other than fleece production, since research is concerned with commercial flocks where fleece quality is not the pay factor. Here is where the small sheepraiser has a real advantage. You can care for your wool and market it to handspinners. You can have more profitable meat lambs by marketing them so selectively that you are getting a retail price rather than the wholesale price that must be accepted by the large commercial grower.

The need for good meat plus prime wool will give you a different goal from that of commercial flock owners. Their standards will still apply, but added to those will be the need for much better wool, with quality and attractiveness that will sell to a specialized market. The result should be both better meat and better wool, justifying a premium price for a premium product.

You can start with a meat breed and cross to get better wool, or you can start with good wool and cross to get a meatier, faster-growing animal. One of the surprising advantages of the longer-wool breeds, apart from their attractiveness to spinners, is the flavor. The U.S. Sheep Station at Dubois, Idaho, notes that wool grade and meat flavor are related. As breeds go from fine to coarse wool, the amount of mutton flavor in the meat decreases, thus enhancing palatability. Tenderness, however, is the result of fast growth to maturity.

Breeding Considerations

The different types of sheep to be considered here can be grouped, roughly, into four classifications: fine wools, medium wools, long wools, and meat types. Following is a short analysis of the advantages and some of the disadvantages of the most commonly available breeds. Although much of this is subject to disagreement, and wool grades even within a breed will differ radically from one flock to another, what follows should prove useful both for crossbreeding and for the tentative selection of a breed for a starting flock. Get additional information before making any final decision.

There are several points you will want to keep in mind. Many experts feel that the ram's breed exerts more influence on the lambs than does the ewe's. This may be true for most factors, but does not pertain to twinning, since the ewe is the one that drops the eggs and makes twinning possible. The important influence of twin rams is on their *daughters*, who will have a significantly higher chance of shedding two eggs at ovulation than daughters of rams with a background of single births.

Qualities such as nervous temperament and mothering instinct are more likely to resemble those of the mother, while outward conformation such as fleece type and color may seem to be more like the father. Some experts feel that lambs are more likely to inherit the weaknesses (to disease and to problems such as prolapse) of the mother, considering that the lamb is supported by the mother's blood during its fetal growth. In early times, the fact of the ram's outward features being reflected in the lamb was attributed to a "nervous influence" on the mother, or the "influence of the imagination." In Biblical days, Jacob was said to have caused his sheep to have lambs that were "ringed, streaked and speckled" by having the ewes look at "peeled rods." Since humans have explained their own strange birthmarks as the effect of fright on the mother during pregnancy, such explanations regarding sheep are not surprising.

Prolificacy is found in many breeds and can often be found in breeds that have other desirable traits. Multiple births can be encouraged by the introduction of highly prolific stock such as Finnsheep, or by selective breeding and keeping only lambs that were twins or triplets.

In crossbreeding for better meat production, look to the larger and faster-growing breeds, because fast and efficient growth is the pay factor in locker-lamb production.

For spinning-wool breeds, there is a great selection to choose from. The favorite fleece of spinners will vary from one area to another, partly by what is available, what is recommended by local teachers, and the temperament of the individual spinners. American spinners seem less opinionated than others about the "right and proper use" for each specific fleece type and are often more concerned with obtaining clean fleeces and a variety of wool types, even blending them for the desired use. This is due in part to a lack of tradition but also to the shortage of good, clean local wool.

In evaluating breed characteristics, keep in mind that wool on the sheep's legs should be considered a disadvantage because it is unusable and makes shearing more time-consuming. Wool on the face, which is very inheritable, is another disadvantage. Tests have shown that an open-faced ewe (with no wool on the face) will raise more lambs and heavier lambs than woolly-faced ewes. Also, open-faced ewes do not suffer wool blindness or collect burrs on the face.

Skin folds, in general, are also undesirable. They do produce a higher grease weight of fleece, but they also mean higher shrinkage. For handspinners, the excessively greasy fleeces are harder to wash. Folds make shearing more tedious, and, since maggots can hatch and thrive in moisture-retaining folds, the folds predispose sheep to fly strike. Skin folds usually indicate a somewhat lower fertility and productivity, according to the U.S. Sheep Industry Development Program. Folds are inheritable and found mainly in fine-wool breeds.

Kemp is an undesirable type of fiber found in some fleeces (more often in certain breeds). These are opaque fibers resembling head and leg hair, usually shorter than the rest of the fleece and with a different physical structure from wool fibers. They are a serious flaw in fleeces for commercial buyers, and handspinners also are not happy with them.

Crimps, which are the waves (natural curl) in wool fibers, increase in number with the fineness of the wool. Long luster wools lack the high number of crimps (or barbs) per inch that are found in fine wools, and this lessens the felting quality of the long wools. Less tendency to felting may be an advantage for some purposes but, obviously, not for feltmaking.

Wool Grading Terms

In order to discuss the wool you hope to produce, you need to know wool grading terms. The three grading systems that have been used traditionally all classify wool by diameter. The oldest is the *blood system*. Next came the *count system*, which was more technical, and then the more recent and more accurate *micron system*.

The blood system was based on the fine wool of the Merino and the Rambouillet. This wool set the standard for fine wool. A cross between a Merino and a coarser-wool breed would result in a coarser wool, which would be "one-half blood." Following this was "three-eighths blood" and "quarter blood" to describe the amount of fine-wool breeding behind a sheep that produced a particular kind of wool. This system is seldom used now.

The count system is most often used by handspinners, and is a more technical classification. The count originally referred to the number of *hanks* of yarn, each 560 yards long, which could be spun from 1 pound of wool top. A 64s (the equivalent of 64 hanks) would yield 35,840 yards (560 yards times 64) or 107,520 feet of yarn. While hanks are seldom mentioned now, the count system does describe yarn in terms that most handspinners can visualize.

The micron system is an industrially accurate measurement of the average diameter of wool fiber. The micron (1/25,000 of an inch) is used as the average diameter measurement. An 80s wool of the count system is 18.1 microns, while a long-wool 36s has an average diameter of 39.7 microns.

In the count system, the higher the number, the finer the fiber. In the micron system, the higher the number, the coarser the wool (see chart on wool grades on page 62).

Corriedales and Dorsets, like these at Wooly Hill Farm, are among the breeds that adapt well to wet weather.

Which Breeds for Which Areas?

The part of the country in which you live, and the general lay of the land, can play a part in breed selection. In general, these are the best choices (of the common sheep breeds) for particular situations:

WET AREA OR WET PASTURE
- Cheviot
- Clun Forest
- Corriedale
- Dorset
- Romney

GOOD PASTURE
- Clun Forest
- Dorset
- Finnsheep
- Hampshire
- Leicester
- Lincoln
- Oxford
- Romney
- Southdown
- Suffolk

DRY AREA OR DRY PASTURE
- Columbia
- Cotswold
- Karakul
- Merino
- Panama
- Rambouillet
- Tunis

ROUGH PASTURE
- Cheviot
- Corriedale
- Karakul
- Merino
- Panama
- Rambouillet
- Targhee
- Tunis

Fine-Wool Breeds

Fine wools are excessively greasy and difficult to card without proper equipment. In the past, they were not generally preferred by the majority of American spinners, but they have recently come into demand and, along with exotic fiber blends, have become extremely popular. Fine wools, if clean and high quality, are now bringing premium prices for handspinning.

Merino and Delaine Merino. This wool is 64s and finer. The body is wrinkled (with skin folds), and the sheep do not thrive in areas of high rainfall because the wetness is hard on their hoofs, making them prone to foot problems, and because their fleeces do not dry quickly, they are susceptible to fleece rot and fly strike. However, these breeds are hardy and can be raised in extremely warm areas under poor feed conditions. They have a long life, and often will breed out of season. They also have good herding instincts and are valuable for commercial raisers, although the lambs lack the good muscling conformation necessary for the best meat production.

Rambouillet. This wool is 60s or finer. Aside from having fewer skin folds than the Merino, the Rambouillet has about the same advantages and disadvantages.

Debouillet. Debouillet wool is 64s or finer, with a heavier fleece weight and less skin wrinkling than Merino or Rambouillet. This sheep originated from a cross of Merino and Rambouillet.

Booroola Merino. A recently developed strain of Australian Merino noted both for high-quality, long-staple, fine wool and for high prolificacy, this may be a breed worth watching in the future. Its multiple lambing results from a single gene that affects ovulation. This is different from the Finnsheep, in which ovulation is controlled by a number of genes. Research regarding the Booroola Merino is being carried on at the U.S. Meat Animal Research Center in Nebraska, where, in the fall of 1983, over thirty purebred Booroola twin lambs were born to Coopworth ewes impregnated by ova shipped there along with five Booroola rams. The lambs are being compared to Finnsheep for reproductive traits as well as for survival ability, growth, and carcass characteristics, with an eye to their usefulness in crossbreeding.

Meat Breeds

Meat breeds are often crossed with the better wool breeds to get a crossbreed that will have some of the best qualities of both. The most favored breeds for this purpose appear to be the Suffolk and Dorset, but for certain qualities others would also be suitable.

Suffolk. Suffolk wool is 54s to 60s, light fleece but light shrinkage. Spinners like the lamb fleeces. The black head and legs are free of wool. Suffolks are easy to shear but have fairly short wool. They are prolific, good milkers, and the rams are aggressive breeders. Good in crossbreeding programs. The lambs have an excellent growth rate and make efficient use of feed.

Dorset. This wool is 50s to 58s, very white, and easy to handle for spinning — good for the Great Wheel. Dorsets have very little wool on the face, legs, and belly. They are good mothers, have very good milking capacity, can breed more than once a year, and live long. Breeding traits and milking ability are usually inherited by crossbreeds. Polled (hornless) Dorsets are the most popular.

Oxford. Oxford wool is 46s to 54s, a very good spinning fleece and longer wool than on most meat breeds. Oxfords have wool on the legs. They are of large size, prolific, and good milkers, and they have fast-growing lambs and a good temperament. Originally, a Hampshire/Cotswold cross.

Cheviot. This wool is 48s to 50s, very light fleece and light shrinkage. The wool is easy to spin but a bit scratchy, and noted for its whiteness. Cheviots have bare legs and heads. They are hardy and prolific, good mothers and efficient grazers, but tend to be nervous and skittery. There are two types: the Border Cheviot, which is smaller, and the North Country Cheviot, larger and with more of a Roman nose.

Hampshire. Hampshire wool is 50s to 58s, a little short for prime spinning. This breed has wool on its legs. Good growth rate, prolific, good milkers, good temperament.

Shropshire. The wool is 56s to 60s, light fleece weight, with light shrinkage. Shropshires have wool on their legs. They are good mothers, and the meaty lambs grow fast to maturity.

Southdown. This wool is 60s to 62s, very light fleece, but light shrinkage. These small-sized sheep have wool on their legs and are good mothers.

Montadale. Montadale wool is 48s to 58s, medium-heavy fleece with light shrinkage. Montadales have bare heads and legs, and are hardy and prolific, with good grazing ability.

Medium-Wool Breeds

Columbia. This wool is 52s to 56s, heavy fleece that dyes well, has light shrinkage, and good spinning quality. Prolific, good milkers, with an especially good growth rate, Columbias were developed from a Lincoln/Rambouillet cross. They are adaptable to both farm and open range, but some say their hoofs are more suited to a dry climate.

Corriedale. Corriedale wool is 50s to 58s, good fleece weight, long and silky wool with good crimp, and desired by many handspinners. Can cross well with meat breeds for good market lambs. The breed is docile and open-faced, with heavily wooled ears, good flocking instincts, and a long life span. Corriedales were developed from a Lincoln/Merino crossing.

Targhee. Targhee wool is 60s to 64s, good fleece weight. This is a hardy breed with good growth, long life, and large size. The prolific ewes lamb easily without help. Resistant to parasites and hoof troubles, adaptable to varied climates and feed. Tolerates heat. Developed in Idaho from one-quarter long-wool breed, three-quarters fine-wool breed.

Tunis. Tunis wool is 56s to 60s, good spinning quality. This is a medium-size sheep, hardy and docile; the ewes are good mothers, prolific, and will breed out of season. The lambs grow fast, and the rams remain fertile in hot weather. Tunis sheep have reddish tan hair on the legs and face, and long ears. Any dark sheep out of this breed could tend toward a good reddish brown.

Clun Forest. This wool is 56s to 60s, good for spinning. The prolific ewes lamb extremely easily without help and are good mothers even as yearlings. Fast growth, rich milk. The breeders' association members will sell a breeding ram only if born a twin or triplet or better. Clun Forest sheep live a long life, are adaptable to all climates, and are good foragers.

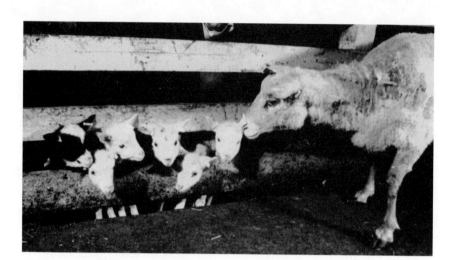

Finnsheep ewe with sextuplets — this is real *prolificacy.*

Panama. Panama wool is 50s to 58s, heavy fleece, good spinning quality. These large-size sheep are hardy, good mothers and milkers, able to tolerate a hot climate, have good muscling, and are hornless.

Finnish Landrace (Finnsheep). Finnsheep wool is 54s to 60s. Although low in fleece production, growth rate, and carcass quality, this is an unusually prolific breed. Good milkers, the ewes lamb easily, breed as yearlings and at almost any time of year. Their high fertility is inherited in crossbreeding. Their low fleece production could be partly the result of body energy going into lambs. Finnsheep need special feed and care during gestation to meet the nutritional needs of their multiple lambs.

Long-Wool Breeds

Thanks to Linda Berry Walker of Woolsedge Wools, who writes a magazine column on sheep breeds, for details on the Border Leicester, Coopworth, Perendale, and Karakul sheep.

Romney. The wool is 40s to 48s, good weight with light shrinkage, denser than in other long-wool breeds. Silky and lustrous, it is easy to spin and prized by many handspinners. Romneys have good feet that require minimal trimming and are resistant to foot rot. The breed is resistant to internal parasites and adaptable to cool, wet climates such as that of the Pacific Northwest and low marshland. These sheep are good mothers, good milkers, sweet-tempered, and faster-maturing than other long-wool breeds. Romneys cross well with other breeds to get other qualities. In 1796 the Royal Agricultural Society of England called the Romney marsh sheep "perhaps the most valuable of any breed of sheep in the world."

Lincoln. Lincoln wool is 36s to 40s, strong and lustrous — an excellent rug yarn and strong weaving warp. The heavy fleece has light shrinkage. This is a large-size animal with no wool on the legs. It grows slowly to maturity and crosses well to add body size and fleece weight to the resulting crossbreed. It likes abundant pasture and can thrive in a cold climate.

Cotswold. This wool is 36s to 40s, in ringlets, long and unusual. The wool makes good warp yarn and is excellent for worsted spinning. This large sheep, which has long tufts of curly wool hanging over its face, can thrive on dry rolling land under poor conditions.

Leicester. The wool is 40s to 48s, with good luster. The softer lambs' fleeces are attractive to handspinners. This breed resembles the Lincoln except that it is smaller, with a short thick neck and wool on the crown of its head and a wool tuft on its forehead.

Border Leicester. This wool is 44s to 48s, easy to prepare and quick to spin. The sheep have bare heads and legs, and are easily sheared. This is a prolific sheep, a good milker that lambs easily without help, and is a very good dual-purpose breed. Will tolerate high rainfall. Good for crossbreeding to get longer wools with a soft luster. With its long slender neck, the Border Leicester presents a very stylish appearance.

Perendale. Perendale wool is 50s to 54s, with a 4- to 5-inch staple. Perendales originated with a cross of Cheviot rams on Romney ewes, developed for the hills of New Zealand. They have clean faces and clean legs, with dense wool inherited from the Romney. They are good foragers and noted for unassisted lambing and vigorous lambs. Inclined to be nervous (a trait inherited from the Cheviot), they should be handled quietly.

Coopworth. This wool is similar in count to Romney, but with the silkiness of the Border Leicester, Coopworths being a cross of the two breeds and their progeny. It is good staple length wool, admired by spinners. The breed association requires mandatory culling, inspection of flocks, and deregistration of ewes not meeting performance requirements. Coopworths are known for prolificacy and easy care.

Karakul. Karakuls produce coarse carpet wool, 8 to 12 inches long. This is a hardy slender animal, producing both fur pelts and wool. The wool is predominately colored, from golden tans and reddish browns to silver blues, grays, and jet black. Fleeces from lambs up to six months old will be soft, with successive shearings more coarse. The fleece has long coarse fibers plus an undercoat of short finer fibers, and tends to mat while on the sheep if subjected to unusual weathering. The Karakul is known as a fur sheep rather than a meat or wool sheep, its primary value being the lamb pelts for fur; the lambs are killed when three to ten days old for Persian lamb or broad tail fur. The tail is not ordinarily docked because it is a food reserve; if the tail is docked, the sheep will need to be provided with more ample food. Karakuls can thrive on scant pasture and low rainfall.

Breeds for Specific Yarns

Here are some general recommendations of the kinds of breeds that are favored by some spinners for particular types of yarn. This list was published in the newsletter of Clotho's Children, a spinning guild in Virginia, and was written by Lisa Sagerholm-Hunter.

◆ *For fine soft yarn:* Merino, halfbreeds, Southdown, or fine Romney
◆ *For thick, bulky yarn:* Cheviot, Perendale, Southdown, or fine Romney

◆ *For shiny yarn:* long-stapled lustrous breeds such as Leicester, Coopworth, or Romney
◆ *For dull yarn:* Cheviot, Southdown, and breeds that lack luster
◆ *For hard yarn:* Lincoln, Leicester, Coopworth, strong Romney, or any coarse- or strong-fleece breed
◆ *For soft yarn (choice will depend on the diameter of the yarn being spun):*
>   *fine yarn:* Merino, halfbreed, or Corriedale
>   *medium yarn:* Corriedale, Perendale, or Romney
◆ *For smooth yarn:* long-stapled fleece from Romney, Leicester, or Coopworth

Black Sheep

For a large-scale commercial operation that will be marketing wool for factory use, white wool will bring by far the best price from a wool pool, but for selling fleeces to handspinners you may want to raise dark sheep. There was a time when dark wool was scarce in the U.S. It was undesirable commercially, and there were not enough spinners to constitute a craft market for it. But times change, spinners now abound, and sheepraisers have responded by raising dark sheep to such an extent that in some places there is a considerable excess of dark wools. But not of *excellent* dark wools. Poor dark fleeces are not easy to sell, but prime ones, nicely sheared and uncontaminated with vegetation, will bring a good price.

The sheep industry has long defined black sheep as any sheep that are not white. The black head and legs that are found on some breeds of white sheep are not part of the fleece, so those are still "white" sheep. However, if dark hairs are part of the sheared fleece, it is not white because it cannot be processed (bleached and dyed) as white wool.

Some dark sheep are mottled, some are spotted. Some have several shades of wool. In general, black-sheep raisers feel that the solid-color fleeces are more desirable to raise than the dark fleeces with wide color variations (except for the Jacob fleeces). Others like distinctive markings — which are somewhat inheritable in a certain bloodline — such as strange markings around the eyes, lighter or darker belly wool, and so on. The genetics of color markings and the genes controlling markings and black sheep color are analyzed in detail in many back issues of *The Black Sheep Newsletter*.

It takes the very *best* of white wool to be as attractive as a medium-quality dark wool. Dirty white wool looks dirtier than dirty dark wool. Many people prefer natural fibers that have not been treated with chemicals, for health or aesthetic reasons, so would rather have undyed dark-sheep colors.

Black sheep do not always run true to type, nor do you always get what you expect to get from crossbreeding, even after carefully studying breed types and bloodlines. You can only look at the results, knowing what you want to keep and what changes you will want to make in the future.

As far as inbreeding is concerned, you need to be guided by results, not by custom or theory. I know one person who sold a dark brown Romney ram that was throwing beautiful offspring. She was concerned about having him too long and getting too much inbreeding, and replaced him with an expensive ram that turned out to produce defective lambs in over 75 percent of her lamb crop. It really pays to be guided mainly by results.

Anyone interested in raising black sheep to obtain handspinning fleeces should subscribe to *The Black Sheep Newsletter* and order as many back issues as are available. This publication is a valuable source of information that is not obtainable elsewhere.

Sheep Management

GOOD FLOCK MANAGEMENT requires a certain amount of basic care and knowledge of sheep — and a great deal of common sense. A healthy flock is the prime consideration toward making a profit.

The First Step: Pregnant Ewes

One of the most important considerations of your breeding program is timing. This matter is taken out of your hands if you are short on space and you pasture your ram with the ewes. If the ram can be kept separately, or just borrowed, you have a choice of when to breed and can, more or less, control the time your lambs are born. Actually, you can only select the date to put the ram in with the ewes and know that lambs will not arrive until at least five months later. A few breeds can be managed to lamb out of season, to obtain three lamb crops in two years. For this, lambs must be fed well enough that they can be weaned between two and three months of age, when they weigh about fifty pounds. The ram can be put with the ewes a week after weaned lambs are separated from the ewes. With breeds that will lamb out of season, this can produce an extra crop of lambs.

Without the use of hormones, you cannot get all the ewes

lambing on the same day or in the same week. Concentrated lambing can be encouraged by a practice known as *flushing*, which gets the ewes into improved condition just before breeding season. Flushing is simply supplementing the ewes' usual summer diet with either fresh pasture or a grain allowance of about half a pound a day, starting seventeen days before the ewes go with the ram. This has a more important result: encouraging the conception of twins. Also, ewes bred in their second or third heat will be more likely to have twins.

The time of the lambing season is of most concern when climate and housing facilities would make early lambing inconvenient. In temperate climates there are advantages to early lambing. The babies are nursing when the mother is still getting grain and hay, which gives her more protein and should result in a better milk supply. It gets the lambs onto the fresh early-spring pasture, gives them good growth before the heat of summer, and lessens the fly problem after docking and castrating. It also gets more lambs to market size in time for customers who want to roast whole lambs for Easter. The ethnic market can make early lambing profitable.

Late lambing also has an advantage. Because of the milder weather, the ewes can conveniently be sheared before lambing, which makes it easier to watch the ewe during the final weeks of pregnancy when it is important to be on the lookout for any sign of prolapse or other problems.

Feeding

In your feeding program, give special attention to the ewe's nutrition while she is pregnant. Consider nutritive value versus bulk. A low-quality hay with insufficient protein cannot be consumed in great enough quantity to nourish the ewes, whose stomach space is crowded by one or more lambs. You need a high-quality protein — that is, grain and/or alfalfa. Any nutritional deficiency at this time could show up in weak lambs and also as tender places in the ewe's wool, making the fleece unsuitable for handspinning and also of less commercial value.

This weak or "tender" wool could also result from a sudden change in the type of grain or feed, so the food change must always be gradual to allow the inner lining of the ewe's stomach to adapt to the difference.

One of the judges at an international sheep shearing contest gave a definite statement about the importance of feed in regard to wool, saying, "Many people overlook nutrition and feeding when it comes to the production of quality wool. It's protein that puts that wool on the lamb."

In addition to feed, good water is important. If sheep are forced to drink poor-quality water, production will be adversely affected. Ewes who do not drink enough water, because of unavailability or unpalatability, will have a smaller milk supply for their lambs. Especially when getting dry feed, sheep need to have lots of water. It is estimated that for every four pounds of dry feed consumed, one gallon of water is needed. This water requirement increases if the temperature rises above 70° F.

Water requirements also increase during late gestation and lactation. With ewes carrying twins, water needs are about 20 percent greater in the fifth month than for ewes carrying single lambs. Ewes that lamb in cold weather may need their drinking water warmed, not just to keep it from freezing, but to encourage consumption, as they prefer water between 40° and 50° F. and will drink less if it varies much from that temperature.

Getting clean wool is the prime consideration of spinners. Much fleece contamination happens because of the method of feeding. Hay racks with slanting dividers will help discourage the sheep from pulling the hay onto each other. Both feed and shelter plans can be found in *Raising Sheep the Modern Way* (see "Sources"). Keeping the feed close to the ground so the sheep has to lower her head to eat seems to minimize a ewe's tendency to back out with a mouthful of hay, most of which ends up in her neighbor's fleece.

In cold, dry climates, some sheepraisers find it convenient to feed hay on the ground next to a fence, changing the feeding place often. With the fence right in front of them, sheep do not step on the feed. This system eliminates much of the neck-wool damage sheep get from rubbing their necks on the slats of hay racks, and reduces the hay and seed contamination of the neck wool. However, in a wet and muddy situation, this type of feeding is not possible.

The Ram's Health

Any disease will weaken a ram, and most diseases will raise his temperature. If a ram has a fever for more than a day or two, it will reduce his sperm production for up to seven weeks.

Be sure you have a regular worming program for your ram, for worm infestation is another stress that weakens him. Check for ticks and lice, and treat him if necessary.

The ram's feet must be sound. Keep them well trimmed, and always check for any sign of soreness or foot abscess. He cannot be virile and aggressive with sore feet. Keep the wool around the ram's organs well sheared to reduce any chance of fly strike on damp or soiled wool.

If you are buying a ram, examine him carefully. Rams with unsound equipment are likely to be unreliable, if not useless. Check the testicles for size, consistency, and abnormalities. A ram's testicles should be large and fairly even in size. Testes size is related proportionately to sperm output. There should be no lumps in either the testes or the cord. Also check the penis. An abscess on the sheath will make a ram less than persistent.

In extremely hot weather, keep the ram in a shady place during the heat of the day, if possible, and put him with the ewes in the evening and leave them together for the night. Heat can reduce sperm count, and extreme heat can cause sterility for several weeks. A sheared scrotum will also keep him cooler.

Shelter

The purpose of a shelter is to protect the sheep (and their fleece) from the weather and/or predators. An adequate shelter need not be closed on all sides to protect from weather; it can have an open side away from the direction of the prevailing wind. It does need secure storage to keep the grain protected from weather and rodents, and to make very sure that the sheep do not accidentally get into the grain, which will result in bloat and probably fatalities. You need a feeding arrangement in the shelter for use in bad weather, and lambing pens (which can be folded and put away for most of the year). The shelter can also provide hay storage, and part of the hay area can be used for the lambing pens in the spring, when much of the hay has been used up. The shelter can also be arranged to give you an area in which you can corral all or some of the sheep when hoof-trimming and worming are needed.

The use of sawdust or wood shavings as bedding is not a good practice because these can get into the fleece. The coarser stems of alfalfa hay, usually rejected by the sheep, work quite well. And you have the satisfaction of using what would otherwise be wasted.

Fencing and Protection from Dogs

The ideal pasture is well fenced to protect sheep from dogs and coyotes, and is free of the burrs and tall weeds that can deposit their seeds in the wool. If the whole pasture cannot be considered safe at night, then a smaller pen around the shelter area is an alternative.

No dog, except those trained as sheepdogs or guard dogs, should ever be allowed near the sheep. Protecting sheep from *all* dogs is the most important way to keep them alive.

If your neighbors' dog is a threat, the best solution I've heard is to give the neighbors' child a lamb; any family that has sheep of their own will certainly not let their dog bother sheep. Alas, if your neighbors have no children, no pasture, or no fences, this is not a solution.

Another means of protection against roaming dogs is to have your own dog, who will sound an alarm at the first sign

Fences, which should be of woven wire such as this one, are not so much to keep sheep in as to keep dogs and predators out.

of trouble or will divert the attention of any trespassing dog. But be sure *your* dog does not get in the habit of chasing sheep, or even playing with them. Play will sooner or later get too rough for the sheep. Old sheep have weak hearts and can't stand chasing, while little lambs are delicate creatures, not able to take rough-and-tumble like puppies. A ewe with a lamb may attack your dog quite violently, causing the startled dog to react and injure the sheep. This would be a normal reaction, and understandable, and the way to prevent it is to keep your dog away from the sheep. Even working sheepdogs are usually tied or penned up at night; they do not work the sheep except under the direction of the shepherd. A sheep guard dog, however, is another matter. Dogs like the Great Pyrenees or Komondor, when properly trained and raised with sheep, do stay with their sheep at night.

Guard dogs are gaining in popularity, with the Komondor and Great Pyrenees most favored. These, if properly raised and trained, are fiercely protective of their flocks, staying with the sheep and blending with them unless a predator comes along. While a well-trained guard dog is usually expensive, it could prevent losses and pay for itself many times over in a few years. For a listing of the raisers of guard dogs, see each issue of *The Shepherd* or *Sheep* (see "Sources").

If you build a pen around a shelter area, you can prevent dogs from digging under the pen by putting barbed wire along the bottom as well as at the top. The fence itself should be of woven wire. A total height of 4 feet is common, but some dogs can jump over that, so a night pen might need to be even higher. If sheep are fed there at dusk and locked in until morning, you will have provided protection for the hours when attack by predators is most likely to happen. If one or two of the sheep have bells, these will alert you when they are being chased. Bells have been used successfully for centuries, even by shepherds who stayed constantly with their flocks. In medieval times, the sheep belonged to the owner who hired the shepherd, but the shepherd provided the bells to be put on the sheep.

New Zealand woven-wire electric fencing is proving effective in protecting sheep from both dogs and coyotes. It is light weight and can be moved from one area to another when you're rotating pastures. This could be installed inside a more permanent fence that is not providing complete protection.

Value of Sheepcovers

If your situation makes it impossible to keep fleeces clean of vegetation, then a coat, or sheepcover, may be the solution. Before the birth of Christ, Romans were using covers on their best sheep to assure clean and unweathered fleeces.

Government research on the subject of sheepcovers has come up with several interesting conclusions. For one thing, sheep wearing plastic sheepcovers are not so prone to predator attack, especially by coyotes. This could make a lot of difference on open range, where coyotes are a constant menace, and also in rural areas, where they have also been known to cause much damage. The statistics also showed a slightly heavier birth weight for lambs born to ewes wearing covers. It has been speculated that this was because the cover had conserved some of the ewes' body energy in cold weather — energy that would have gone into keeping warm, but instead

Sheep at The River Farm wearing woven plastic sheepcovers. The sheep in the left foreground has been uncovered for shearing.

could be converted into lamb weight. There was also a very slight increase in fleece weight on coated sheep. The University of Wyoming has estimated that the use of coats, in cold winters, could result in 13 percent longer fleece-staple length.

How long the cover will last depends not just on the material it is made of but on the circumstances where it is in use. Canvas covers wear well in most surroundings, but the cost is high. Plastic-coated fabric covers usually last more than one season. Plastic covers that are not fabric-backed tear easily on sharp brush or fences.

Many different sheepcovers are now available (see "Sources") and are made especially for protecting handspinning fleeces. They do not cover as much of the sheep as the expensive canvas "show blankets," as they are to be worn all year-round and allow for breeding, lambing, and nursing. A little bit of the fleece is thus left uncovered and gets dirty. The prime portions of the fleece, however, will be kept wonderfully clean. Most sheepcovers come in three to five different sizes, to fit almost any sheep. The flock at The River Farm in Virginia has been protected by these covers since 1979, and the farm's owners are most happy with the resulting fleeces. The covers are put on the sheep right after shearing and left on until the next shearing, twelve months later. A few sheep, about one in twenty, will act crazy for about the first five minutes, because the covers are woven plastic and rattle when new. Most covers are tough and can be expected to last a year or more in most situations. The elastic tends to break down, though, so if the elastic is replaced it gives additional life to the garment.

Initial research on sheepcovers began in Australia (where they're called *rugs* or *coats*) in about 1960, with the goal of reducing the amount of vegetable and foreign contamination of the wool clip. Over 20,000 sheep were involved in the research.

Covers tested were made from a woven polyethylene fabric similar to that of the covers used by The River Farm — a fabric that contains a high concentration of ultraviolet inhibitors to reduce solar degradation of the wool on the sheep's back. (That part of the wool is particularly prone to protein breakdown in the fibers when exposed to temperatures of 90° F. and above.)

The sheep's head is pulled through the front of the cover and the back legs are slipped through side straps. The belly, legs, head, and a small portion of the hindquarters are the only unprotected areas. That portion of the hindquarters is unlikely to get any burrs in it anyway, as the sheep does not usually back into burrs. Elastic inserts fitted through the neck and back allow the cover to stretch as the wool grows. However, if you are using these covers for young, growing sheep of a long-wool breed, watch out for covers becoming tight after about eight months' growth of wool. The sheep may need to be fitted with the next larger size for the rest of the year.

There are additional advantages from sheepcovers beyond the cleanliness of the wool. The covers produce a more even year-round skin temperature, which in general leads to healthier animals. Also, by using sheepcovers straight after winter or early-spring shearing, you minimize the risks of deaths from thermal shock. Being of a woven nature, the wool is able to "breathe," so even in the hottest climates the wool will not sweat under the covers.

Because they partially protect wool from rain, the covers

minimize fleece rot and skin diseases, according to the Australian research. The incidence of fly strike is also reduced, probably because the sheep are healthier.

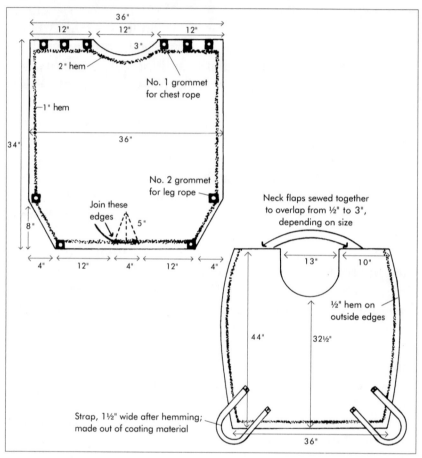

Two styles of sheepcover for keeping the fleece clean. Since the cost of ready-made covers is the main factor in discouraging their use, you might want to try making one. Number-10 duck or canvas has generally proved satisfactory, although subject to wear if kept on the sheep for a full year. Some plastics also work well, but cotton or number-12 burlap does not.
Left: *University of Wyoming design. Dimensions are for sheep measuring 31 inches or less from mid-neck to dock. Enlarge for bigger sheep.*
Right: *To make this coat in the largest size, make leg loops 27 inches long and overlap neck flaps ½ inch. For medium size, make 24-inch loops with 1½-inch neck-flap overlap. For small, make 24-inch loops with 3-inch neck-flap overlap. Attach loops by stitching them down.*

Dark sheep, which tend to absorb more heat than white sheep, benefit from sheepcovers in additional ways. The covers, being light-colored, reflect a certain amount of summer heat, and black sheep with covers can often be seen grazing while dark sheep without covers are seeking shade. Furthermore, the covers reduce the fading and color changes of the wool tip. Ordinarily, as much as 25 percent of the total staple length could be lost with badly weathered tips, and the covers reduce this weathering.

Most Australian research was with Merino sheep. With Border Leicesters, the long, dense, coarse wool tends to become cross-fibered or somewhat matted, and this would probably also happen with mohair goats.

If you wonder how sheepcovers would affect the fleece of your particular breed, try two for a year, and compare the covered fleeces with uncovered ones.

The sheepcover pattern shown here originated at the University of Wyoming for do-it-yourselfers. For material, the University suggests number-10 duck or canvas. In making your own, you could try several different materials to see what would work best in your particular climate.

Parasites and Health

Ticks can cause stains in the wool, damage the skins and thus lower the value of a tanned pelt, and sap the strength of the sheep even to the point of anemia. While there are many high-powered chemicals that can be used, I favor rotenone (a plant-derived insecticide that is safe enough to use on garden vegetables until the day before you eat them; see formula and directions for use, page 173). Getting rid of ticks should take only two applications of rotenone, at the most. If sheep are treated immediately after shearing this kills all the *live* ticks. It may eliminate *all* the ticks, as the tick eggs (pupa) are not really next to the skin, but are fastened to the wool about half an inch from the skin, so most are removed in shearing. To make really sure, you can treat the sheep again after twenty-four days, when the eggs would have hatched but before the new ticks could in turn lay more eggs. Once you have eliminated ticks from your flock, the only way you can get them again is to bring in a strange sheep, or loan out your ram. These ticks do not come from the grass, and they are not wood ticks; they can come only from another sheep. All your sheared sheep as well as their lambs should be treated at one time so that the ewes don't acquire a new batch of ticks from untreated lambs.

Internal parasites (worms) are harder to identify than ticks and never totally eradicated. There are quite a few varieties of stomach worms, and they may require different medications. In general, the all-purpose wormers will take care of most. Get a wormer that is safe for lambs and pregnant ewes. Read the directions — they will tell you not only the correct dosage, but also the time that must elapse between treatment and the slaughter of meat animals.

A regular program of worming is needed to keep sheep in good health. Extreme parasite infestation can weaken sheep so that they are subject to other diseases due to their run-down condition. In advanced cases, sheep have severe diarrhea and become anemic. One other symptom is "bottle jaw," a swelling of the neck under the jaw. Overgrazing of pastures may necessitate even more frequent wormings than the customary four times a year.

Inherited Fleece Defects

Some of the factors that lower the value of a fleece, both for manufacturers and for handspinners, are genetic, and to some extent they can be minimized or prevented by a careful program of culling. Some of these defects are

◆ **Hairy fibers.** These are more common in the coarser wool breeds, especially in the britch (rump) area. For interesting yarn, these fibers can sometimes be useful and are not as undesirable for handspinners as for use in industry. These are medullated fibers, with a different kind of core from the fibers in the rest of the fleece. They do not dye well, are more angular, and, when spun, do not bend and curve the same as the rest. Research has determined that production of medullated fibers increases for a short period after shearing, especially after close shearing, but can be prevented by high shearing or use of sheepcovers.

◆ **Kemp.** This is an opaque fiber found in some fleeces, as, for example, in the Scottish Blackface and Welsh Mountain breeds. While generally rejected by industry, the kempy fleeces are good for special effects in tweed yarn and fabric, as they dye differently. Kemp fibers have a sharp pointed tip, and are flatter than normal fibers. They are shorter than the rest of the fleece fibers, and almost straight, although some may have abrupt kinks.

◆ **Stringy yolk.** When a waxy secretion produced by hyperactive skin glands combines with suint (sheep sweat), the result is *yolk*. When yolk dries along the wool fibers, it is difficult to dissolve and wash out of the fleece in a home scouring facility. This is considered to be a genetic fault, but is not as bothersome in mill production as in handspinning use.

◆ **Dark fibers in white fleeces.** This is of prime concern to manufacturers, as dark hairs will not bleach or dye, and can show up as flaws in a finished piece of pale-colored fabric, causing it to be downgraded in quality, with a consequent loss of profits. However, if there are sufficient dark fibers, the fleece could be of special value for handspinning into unusual off-white yarn.

Fleece Defects Caused by Environment or Inadequate Care

While some fleece flaws can be controlled to a certain degree by breeding, others are due to climate, and some, to a great extent, simply by careless or improper management. Here are some of the nonhereditary problems:

◆ **Tender wool.** While a tender fleece, having one or more weak places in the fibers, can be caused by a deficiency of copper in the diet, it is most commonly caused by stress. The stress can be climate, such as a summer drought or an extreme of temperature, or poor winter feeding. It could also be illness and fever, a hormone imbalance, severe internal parasites, old age, predator attack, or pregnancy. While there are some normal seasonal periods of slight change in fiber strength (density), the months of pregnancy cause the most change. Shearing just before lambing will usually cut the fibers near the weakest point, which is an advantage in minimizing the effects of this minor tenderness.

◆ **Steely wool.** This is almost always traced to a copper deficiency. It shows up in dark sheep as a loss of much of their pigmentation, but should not be confused with the gradual year-by-year graying of the fleece that is typical of most dark sheep. Steely wool has poor crimp and a shiny appearance that leads to the name, and suffers much breakage in use due to low tensile strength. Copper deficiency in the diet also causes debilitated sheep, which lowers wool production, but copper supplements must be used cautiously, as too much copper added to the diet can produce copper poisoning.

◆ **Cotted or matted wool.** Poor feeding helps cause this problem; other causes are stress, and frequent wetting and drying of the fleece during seasons of alternating dry and rainy days. The problem is greater with old sheep, where more fibers may be shed during the year. Cotting can also be caused by insufficient production of wool grease due to illness. In mill terms, the fiber entanglement is commercially classed as *soft* or *hard*, depending on its severity, and this fiber suffers much breakage during mill picking and carding. Matted fleece is apt to be stained, because matting interferes with the normal yolk movement along the fibers. Some fiber shedding occurs in winter, due to weather factors, and early spring shearing can minimize its matting effect. Double-coat fleeces such as Karakul can become quite matted when the sheep are kept in an overly wet climate.

◆ ***Weathered wool.*** Weathering and fleece rot are caused by alternating periods of rain and intense sunlight. It is a regional problem, although fleece rot can occur without the sunlight factor, especially in the less compact type of fleeces. Weathering can cause some loss of wool, especially along the backbone, and can also make the wool more brittle, lacking strength along the entire length of fiber. Excessively weathered tips can often be identified without even being touched, as they appear matted and have a stuck-together appearance as though the tips were muddy. These weathered tips will dye differently, and usually break off during processing. The weathered fleeces will felt better than good wool. In any case, much weathering can be prevented by breeding for a more compact fleece, or just by the use of sheepcovers.

◆ ***Stained wool.*** Other than dung and urine stains, most stains are caused by controllable conditions. Brands and marking paint should be "scourable," but some are still indelible enough to be a problem to handspinners who want to wash their wool gently. Some sheep dip can stain the wool and requires a commercial bleach to remove it. Arsenic burn, another kind of stain, can occur from some dipping fluids. The arsenic is absorbed through breaks in the skin and through shearing nicks, causing a kind of skin destruction so that the skin dries in a hard band on the wool fibers.

Severe tick infestation can also stain the wool. And hot humid temperatures before shearing are said to be the primary cause of canary-yellow staining. In any case, a few unusually hot days just before shearing can sometimes cause some yellowing of the fleece from the yolk, and this becomes more permanent if the fleece is kept too long without washing.

Shearing

If you have only a few sheep, consider shearing your own. This allows control over the quality of the shearing, since you can go slow and avoid second cuts. The sheep need not all be done the same day. Since you do not have to fit into a shearer's schedule, you have the convenience of doing it when you want. Take your time in skirting the fleeces, do a good job of each one, and then package the wool attractively if you plan to sell it to spinners. With nice wool and a healthy sheep, shearing can be very gratifying. There is also, of course, a saving in money.

For your purpose, hand shears could be the thing to use. They cost less, offer less temptation to hurry, and are easy to sharpen and less unnerving. For suppliers of hand shears, see "Sources."

If you decide to hire a shearer, mention to him (or her) that you are most concerned about the fleece, not the appearance of the sheep. Ask if he can shear with a very minimum of second cuts. It would be worth paying extra to get a special job. Sheep shearers have explained that speed is necessitated by two factors: the shearers are paid per sheep and have to hustle to make money, and the average farmer would never hire them again if they were slow and careful, because their slowness would be seen as evidence of lack of skill. Do not fall into the trap of equating speed with the best possible job.

Prepare ahead for the shearer, and have all your facilities ready. The sheep must be penned up and must be dry. It will be your responsibility to have the area clean, and to sweep off the floor or tarp after each sheep.

Commercial sheepraisers have always been instructed to shear dark and white sheep separately and sweep off the floor between shearings. This is done to protect the white wool. For handspinning fleeces, it works to protect *both* kinds of wool. Spinners do not want dark wool in their white fleeces, and do not want to find white wool in their dark fleeces.

There was a good article in the December, 1983 issue of *SpinOff* that should be required reading for people who raise wool for spinners. It was a fleece-evaluation guide, by the point system, intended for use in judging fleeces at sheep shows. Under "What to Look For" was a very straight-to-the-point statement that said, "A prime handspinning fleece will be virtually free of vegetation, stains and second cuts. The presence of all or any of these requires extra work by the handspinner and thus lowers the value of the fleece."

See chapter 5, "Preparing and Selling Raw Wool," for more information on shearing.

Skirting and Rolling a Fleece

Skirting is the removal of a strip about 3 inches wide from the edges of the shorn fleece. For skirting and rolling fleece, a special table can be made onto which each fleece can be thrown (cut side down) after it is sheared. The table should have a slatted top to permit tags and any second cuts to fall through. Working quickly, you could skirt each fleece while

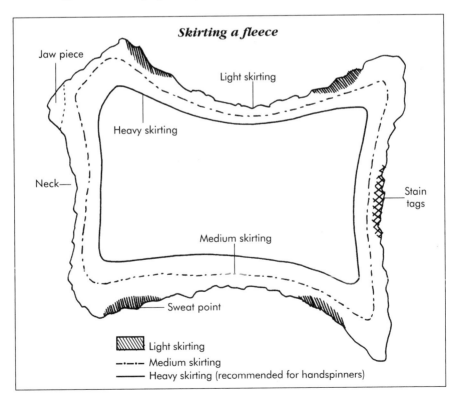

Skirting a fleece

Jaw piece

Light skirting

Heavy skirting

Neck—

Stain tags

Medium skirting

Sweat point

Light skirting
—·—·— Medium skirting
——— Heavy skirting (recommended for handspinners)

the next fleece is being shorn, taking off a strip about 3 inches wide around the edge of the whole fleece. This should remove the belly wool, neck wool, leg wool, and manure tags. The rest of the fleece, if not full of seeds and vegetation, could be of interest to spinners.

For spinners, fleeces do not need to be rolled and tied, as spinners will want to look at them before buying. Most spinners would rather that the fleeces be layered in boxes, with newspaper in between. (Newspaper has the reputation of being somewhat repellent to moths, a claim that is interesting but not proven.) The disadvantage of rolling and tying the fleece is that it presses second cuts so firmly into the fleece that they will not shake out easily. And, it is more difficult for a spinner to inspect the fleece before purchasing.

Fleece-Rolling Method Advised by the
Australian Woolgrower's Manual

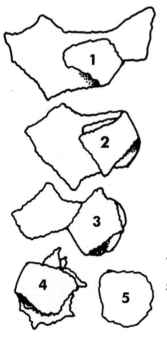

1. Lay unskirted fleece cut side down on a table. On the side nearest you, lightly skirt the fleece from midflank to the center of the britch, then tear the fleece about 2 feet from the center of the britch toward the back. Fold skirted section all the way across the back as shown, making sure the section lies flat.
2. Lean across the table, draw the second britch section over the first, then skirt that section.
3. Again starting at midflank, skirt lightly to the top center of the neck, then tear the fleece 2 feet toward the back. Fold skirted neck section over the britch sections, far enough to expose shoulder wool. Be sure the section lies flat and even.
4. Lean over the table, draw the other neck section across, and skirt it.
5. Turn surplus edges underneath the center of the fleece. You will have four cut sides showing, with the back wool on the bottom. Tie in both directions with paper twine.

The method of fleece-rolling can differ from one country to another. The acceptable method of rolling in the U.S. is to spread out the fleece, cut side down, and fold the side edges in toward the middle. Then the neck edge is folded toward the center. Last, the fleece is rolled inward from the tail end to make a compact package. With *paper* twine it is tied around in one direction, then the twine is crossed and tied around in the other direction, and knotted securely. A slipknot in the starting end of the twine will make it easy to cinch tight.

Another fleece-rolling method, sometimes used in Australia, is for the sides to be folded inward, then the fleece rolled from the tail end, and the neck wool twisted and elongated into a "tail" that is then wrapped around the whole bundle.

A century ago, fleeces were folded into an oblong package, then compressed in a folding trough before tying.

An alternative to these, suggested in the *Woolgrower's Manual*, published in Australia in 1937, said that the orthodox method of rolling had a tendency to expose a greater part of the back wool with the shoulder, and that when the first layer of wool was torn open it revealed the "top side," which did not enhance the appearance. The method the manual suggested, illustrated here, was said to be faster and to give a superior appearance to the wool.

Selling Breeding Stock

Both purebred and purebred registered stock are in demand, although the amount of demand will depend on the breed of sheep. If you have an unusual breed, or just one that is scarce in your region, this gives a potential for selling your sheep for breeding. White sheep of the long-wooled breeds are currently bringing a high price, but it is hard to predict if this is just a temporary trend. Dark sheep with really good-quality wool will bring above-average prices in certain locations. Once a lot of them are available in an area, the laws of supply and demand may start lowering the market price.

How do you sell breeding stock? By working hard at it.

Some sheepraisers go to all of the county fairs within a reasonable traveling distance. Winning ribbons can be a help in getting your name established. The amount of money that is usually awarded at fairs may not be enough to pay for the gasoline costs, but the blue ribbons lend a certain prestige.

Join sheep associations and be aggressive about promoting your own breed and about sheep in general. Be sure that the county agent knows what sheep you have, how well you care for them, and that they are definitely for sale as choice breeding stock. If your agent is interested, you may be able to get together a sheep-flock tour for people who are curious about the possibility of keeping sheep and know little about it.

Selling breeding stock automatically necessitates more record-keeping than normally required. A customer will want the history of the lamb, a record of shearing weights of its mother and father (usually called the *dam* and *sire*), weight when it was born, the rate of gain, whether it was a twin, and if either of its parents were twins. Think of the statistics that you would want if you were making the purchase.

If you have dark sheep for sale, advertise in *The Black Sheep Newsletter*, which has a fairly large and really live-wire circulation. People looking for special breeds of dark sheep are always going through the ads, hoping to find the breeds of their preference. You may have it. There is also a national colored-wool growers association that is active in some parts of the U.S. It would be a good idea to contact dark-sheep raisers in your own area to find out what their experience has been with this association, and whether they feel joining it would be helpful for you.

Quite a few of the major sheep-breed registry associations are now registering dark sheep of their breeds, and others are considering it. If your sheep are purebred, of a breed that will register dark sheep, you should register with that particular breed association.

The people who buy wool from you may be potential sheep customers. If they have an acre or two, mention to them how nice it is to have sheep, how well the sheep keep down the grass, how friendly they can be, and how nice it is to have your own wool.

Anyone with a fenced field could be a potential sheep customer. One way such a person could get started would be by getting a couple of lambs of weaning age and keeping them on the pasture all summer, then putting them in the locker in the fall, about the time the grass gives out and feed would be required. After that, this person might decide to keep a couple of ewes all year-round, with the pasture supporting both ewes and their lambs in the summer, after which the lambs would go into the freezer and the two ewes be kept on the pasture all winter. Discourage a customer from keeping more sheep than the pasture will accommodate all year-round.

An annual open house is a good way to acquaint people in your area with what you are doing and what you have to sell. They may buy locker lamb the first time and sheep the next. Send out invitations and a notice to your local newspaper. Leave fliers at feed stores, laundromats, and any place where there is a bulletin board. Advertise the open house in the farm column. If it is at the same time every year, such as the last weekend in May, people will look forward to it, and plan on attending. Make sure it is an interesting day for them. Invite spinners, and see if they would put on a spinning demonstration in exchange for wool.

Selling Locker Lambs

A meat breed is more suitable for locker lambs due to the body conformation, the meaty look, and the quick growth. However, with ample pasture, good milking ewes, and creep feeding, lambs of comparable weight can be produced by what are normally considered wool breeds.

Before selling a lamb for meat, discuss with a new customer the relationship between the live and dressed weight of the animal, how many pounds of meat to expect after processing, and something about the various cuts of lamb. You don't want customers to be unhappy when they find that they get about 50 percent of the live weight as meat, wrapped and frozen. So they will know they are coming out ahead financially, suggest they go to the supermarket and take a look at the price being charged for different cuts. Tell them to let the processor know how to cut the meat for their families' sizes and eating habits. They should know that they have a choice of stew meat or ground meat, of roasts or boneless cubes for kebabs, and that the shoulder can be cut into roasts or into shoulder steaks. It is good to tell them the special herbs that will enhance the flavor of lamb, and that the cooking temperature should usually be a little lower than for beef. Some sellers give a lamb cookbook with every locker lamb they sell. A good cookbook is available from *The Black Sheep Newsletter* (look under cookbooks in "Sources").

One of the advantages of selling locker lambs to people in your own area is the possibility that the lamb can be sheared before it goes to the locker. If you sell it at locker age, you obviously can shear it then. When the customer buys it at weaning age and raises it on his own pasture until fall, you might still get the fleece; if you have the means for transporting sheep and the lamb buyer has only a car, you could offer to pick up the lamb at the specified time and take it to the slaughterhouse (shearing it first, of course). The customer is usually happy that you can use the fleece.

There is also a specific market for "organically grown" locker lamb. When you are feeding whole grains rather than pelleted ration, you know exactly what you are feeding so you can tell your customer that the lambs are not getting additives and hormones. If you have a good pasture that does not need chemical fertilizer, this is a plus. If your sheep get unsprayed apples from your orchard, tell the customer. Keep your flock free from ticks, using only rotenone (if necessary) rather than any of the chemicals that require waiting two to four weeks before it is safe to eat the meat. Point out that rotenone is the powdered root of a tropical plant, not a manufactured chemical, and can be used on garden vegetables until the day before you eat them. Your local health-food store may be willing to put up a little "Organic Lamb for Sale" sign and refer customers to you. A package of lamb chops, from time to time, could make the store owners more agreeable.

Do not overlook the ethnic market for lambs. Greeks and mid-Eastern nationalities will be interested, particularly at Easter, and frequently at other times when you have lambs available.

There is one other option you may want to consider, especially when a lamb is going to the locker and does not have a fleece long enough to warrant shearing. Pick up the pelt as soon after slaughter as possible, and salt and dry it for tanning. Home tanning takes time and effort, but many sheepraisers are doing it successfully. (Or the skin can be sent away for tanning; look under tanning in "Sources.") To prepare the fresh skin, apply 2 pounds of granular salt per lambskin, about 5 pounds on a large sheepskin. Salt draws the moisture out of the skin. If the slaughterhouse has made cuts in the middle of the skin, you can use it after tanning to make shearling articles. If it is a good uncut skin, you may want to sell it as a whole tanned pelt (see chapter 8, "Income-Producing Angles").

When delivering the lamb to the slaughterhouse for a customer who has been raising it all summer, you may not want to mention tanning in front of the customer — the customer may decide to keep the skin.

"Lamb" is not the only meat product from sheep. The general public may have a poor impression of mutton, but farm-raised mutton, having been fed with hay and grain, is delicious. The larger carcass yields large steaks and chops and leg of mutton. A good portion can be cut as ground meat, useful in any of your hamburger recipes, but leaner. For my part, I am happy to sell the lambs and keep the mutton for my own use.

A slow cooker (such as a Crock-Pot) is ideal for mutton. The following is a good recipe from *My Secret Cookbook* and can be used for lamb neck slices, shanks, steaks, and any cuts of mutton.

Oregon Lamb

3 tablespoons flour
1 teaspoon dry mustard
1 teaspoon salt
½ teaspoon coarsely ground pepper
4 lamb shanks, split
or
3 to 4 pounds lamb neck, sliced
or
2 to 3 pounds lamb steaks, chops, or shoulder roast
Oil for browning
One 10½-ounce can consommé
One 10½-ounce can condensed cream of mushroom soup
1 tablespoon Worcestershire sauce
1 tablespoon Kitchen Bouquet
⅛ teaspoon garlic powder or 2 cloves crushed garlic
½ teaspoon curry powder
½ cup white wine

4 to 6 servings rice, noodles, or potatoes

Put flour, mustard, salt, and pepper in a bag, add meat, and shake to coat. Brown coated meat in hot oil in a nonstick skillet and place in a slow-cooking pot. Combine all remaining ingredients, except rice or pasta, and add to the meat. The sauce should cover about three quarters of the meat. Cook 1 hour on high, then cook on low for 6 to 8 hours, or until the meat is extremely well done. Serve at once, or pour off all liquid and chill it until the fat can be skimmed off. When ready to serve, pour the degreased liquid back over the meat and reheat. Serve on rice or pasta. Serves four to six.

Selling Wool
without Shepherding

A COTTAGE INDUSTRY based on processing wool is usually built on easy access to the raw material, but this doesn't mean that you must keep sheep. For those who are unable to raise their own animals, or do not wish to raise them, there is the option of staying involved with wool by *buying* the fleece required for the end use. It is probably just as rewarding to selectively purchase your wool for resale or further manufacturing as it is to raise your own stock.

Purchased wool can be resold in several ways: as is; sorted and packaged; washed and resold; further processed into carded wool for spinning; or as a finished product such as yarn, yardage, clothing, handmade felt, or comforters.

Who should consider making an income from wool? Primarily, individuals or groups who want a home enterprise. This would include craftspeople like spinners, dyers, quilters, and feltmakers; sheep-shearers with access to wool; and owners of shops with related interests, such as craft shops, yarn shops, gift shops, weavers' shops, and yardage shops that sell cotton quilt fabrics. Or, perhaps co-ops that both use and sell wool, spinning and weaving guilds that want to raise money, family farms where children and adults can work together, or a Junior Achievement type of group. People who get involved

Kay Fielding of Custom Colors in Nevada, a wool-based cottage industry that does not involve shepherding. Kay and her husband dye and card color and fiber blends for sale by mail, wholesale and retail.

with wool are more likely to succeed if they like working with their hands and are creative. For all these people, there is ample opportunity to develop a small enterprise with fairly low capital demands, based on wool.

Advantages of Buying Wool

Time is on your side when you are just buying the wool. Not being a sheep owner, you have more time to spend in creative production and marketing. Without sheep, you may have more flexibility and freedom, be able to travel to weaving conferences and fairs to sell your wares, or have time to take a vacation without worrying about leaving sheep unattended. Sheep care requires a lot of time, as any sheep owner would tell you.

Some of the advantages of buying, rather than raising, wool are

◆ **Low overhead.** If business is slack, there are few expenses to worry about until business picks up and you need to buy.

◆ **Choice of wool.** You can choose the wool most desired by your market. This may change from year to year, and you can change the type you purchase.

◆ ***Wool quality.*** You can work with only the top level of quality, once you establish your sources. The quality of the end product can then be higher, and you do not have to waste time dealing with skirtings.

◆ ***Cost of material.*** Don't imagine that the sheepraiser is getting the wool "free" or even cheap. It costs the grower almost as much to grow the wool as it costs you to buy. Sheepraisers depend on wool sales, in most instances, to help break even on the cost of raising sheep and depend on meat sales to make a profit.

◆ ***Efficiency of operation.*** For the person who likes operating in a businesslike manner, the nongrowing aspect of the undertaking can be controlled with greater efficiency than the affairs of the grower, who has to contend with the seasonal vagaries of nature.

◆ ***Product flexibility.*** The flock owner who wishes to make a change in wool type has at least one or two years' lag and the expense of obtaining new stock, while the nongrower can do it with a letter or a phone call.

◆ ***Objectivity.*** The sheep owner is very close to his own animals and his own wool and not always as free to judge wool impersonally as the nongrower because of the commitment to his situation.

◆ ***Freedom from involvement.*** The nongrower is free of the distractions of raising animals. The person who has sheep is like a mother with children; they are never out of mind completely. Sheep growers cannot ignore the requirements of their flocks.

◆ ***Creativity.*** Not being concerned with animals can leave you free to imagine and produce more unusual and exciting products, and have the time to concentrate on design and production.

◆ ***Option of part-time work.*** Most home businesses start off as part time. Ideally, you need someone on the premises at all times if you are raising sheep, which, for an employed person or couple, would be impossible. However, evenings and weekends give you the kind of time needed to start building up a cottage industry based on *purchased* raw materials. This could eventually lead to the kind of income that allows more time at home, if desirable.

The In-between Situation: A Few Sheep

Some of the people who have only a few sheep might appear to be using them simply to make their businesses more attractive to customers, or more picturesque, or more interesting to themselves while they are buying a great proportion of the wool that they use or sell. In fact, a flock too small to support the business is often the result when a person has started a wool enterprise on a small scale and then finds that the potential market for the wool product far outreaches the homegrown supply of wool.

In a situation where there is space and pasture for only a few sheep, it is possible to have it both ways. Keeping too many sheep in a small area would not only be expensive because of the cost of purchased feed but, in addition, overgrazing can predispose sheep to diseases and severe internal-parasite problems. The alternative is to keep just a few sheep, in good health and requiring a minimum of care time, and to buy enough wool to supply the changing needs of business.

Reselling Wool

Small spinning shops are now buying many tons of New Zealand and Australian wool just to resell, without any further processing. Mail-order businesses, after locating reliable suppliers in either of those two countries, or locally, are also buying and reselling, both wholesale and retail.

A person buying wool to process and resell can usually double the income that would come from selling just grease wool. While this profit is not without time spent in the processing, it does give a higher rate of return on the investment in the raw material.

Financial Considerations When Getting Started

For someone who already has sheep, starting a sheep-based cottage industry is a logical development. For someone who does not already own sheep, it is easier, quicker, and cheaper to start by purchasing good wool than by purchasing sheep and preparing a place for them.

The cost of starting up a small wool venture without sheep can be fairly nominal. The safest way to start is very small with minimal equipment such as a good table-top picker and a drum carder (see chapter 10). The smaller equipment is not wasted when you decide to get larger tools, since it is still useful for small tasks and has a resale value. Many craftspeople have started out with hand equipment and gradually worked up sufficient volume to justify and afford larger equipment, as more efficient machinery was needed and the business could support it. While hand tools are very labor-intensive, they give the opportunity to measure the demand and to work up a product.

Deluxe table-top drum carder with optional motorpack.

One important aspect of starting this kind of a small business is your marketing and management ability — business management and money management. Not all available money should be tied up in equipment. Funds should be available to buy materials if a good buy should present itself. A large purchase of choice wool at a good price, for example, could allow the option of a roll-over of a portion of that wool immediately without any labor invested in processing. This profit, without the time spent in working on the wool, is an important type of cash flow. And small diversifications such as this are good business.

Reliable Wool Sources

In buying wool, one of the main concerns is locating and maintaining a steady supply of high-quality wool. The level of quality will depend on how astutely you buy, and on the person selling the wool. To get a steady supplier, you need to pay that person a fair price. Develop a good relationship so you are welcome the next year.

Even if you *could* get all your wool from one source, you should keep other options open and probably spread business around a little in case your supplier has problems. Because you are buying, you are less vulnerable than the person raising sheep, who is subject to environmental hazards of weather, predators, and sheep diseases. Since your suppliers are at risk from these problems, this makes it important not to rely completely on a single source.

Initially, there are problems in buying by mail, as there is no assurance of quality unless you know someone who buys from that source and can show you the wool. Samples are useful but usually supplied from the best part of the fleece. However, there are many reputable sellers whose samples are a true representation of the product being offered. Once you establish good sources of supply, you can usually rely on continuity of quality.

Buying Quality Wool in Quantity

While the best quality may cost more than wool that is not so nice, you may be able to bargain for a better price by taking larger quantities at a time. The grower might like selling the whole clip, or the best of it, all at one time and having the cash for it, and then marketing the lower quality and the skirtings for a lower price. The alternative for the grower would be to keep the best on hand and hope to sell it, a pound or a fleece at a time, to individual spinners.

In looking for quality, most purchasers of raw wool ask for clean well-skirted fleeces of a specific wool type and length that is suited to their needs.

Creating Markets

Many established enterprises could add your wool-related products to their businesses. Could your products be incorporated into a nonwool field in which you are already involved, or with which you were previously associated? Think creatively about this.

Successful large businesses diversify, improve, upgrade, and continually offer new or better products, more attractively packaged. This is an accepted concept and can be applied in a small situation. What is needed is an inventive testing of the market to identify new opportunities, and an imaginative new presentation of a standard product, to stimulate customers' interest.

Those who *buy* their wool are in a better position to evaluate new materials and products than a person who is tied to a flock. Because they are researching the marketplace for better quality and greater variety, nongrowers stumble across a lot of new ideas just through contacting so many people. They may accidentally find things they were not looking for or expecting to find. We all know of businesses that have grown out of a mistake, an unusual idea, or an accidental happening. The important thing is to recognize an opportunity, or to take an unrelated idea and modify it to apply to wool products and their merchandising.

Value of the Unusual Finished Product

Although it's rewarding to develop a market for what you most enjoy doing, try not to settle for doing only what you know the public will buy. In the craft field, individuality always brings a higher price than standardization. This need not be one-of-a-kind items, but a certain exclusiveness can be rewarding both financially and emotionally. Originals are valued.

Avalene McCaul of Indian Springs Farm, dyeing a batch of wool that, depending on the purchaser, could end up in combination with anything from leather to jewelry to basketry.

There is not much point in imitation of mass-produced articles *unless* you can do it with a unique touch, a recognizable higher quality, a texture the factory cannot duplicate, or irregularities with a special human touch. The person who is buying the raw material and converting it into a salable product is more likely to develop an expertise in incorporating exotic materials or suitable natural things, such as feathers, grasses, wood products, leather, or other unusual decorations, such as antique jewelry and buttons, or handcrafted buckles and bangles.

There are wonderful possibilities in combining materials — soft leather-and-felt combinations, or

Ultrasuede with felt and fabric. In Florida, for example, handspun yarn is much used in handmade basketry. An unusual use of wool, an unusual presentation of the product, or an unexpected combination of materials can be exciting for both you and your customers.

Preparing and Selling Raw Wool

TO SELL RAW WOOL PROFITABLY takes knowledge and understanding of the market. Whether you are raising wool or buying it for resale, it is essential to have a thorough technical understanding — to know more about wool than either your supplier or your customers.

Analysis of the Competition

If you're selling raw wool, the competition to be concerned about is not the neighbor who raises sheep but the tremendous quantities of wool shipped into both the United States and Canada, particularly from Australia and New Zealand. It is well known that a majority of the grease wool used by American factories is imported. Manufacturers turn to imported wools because they cannot find what they want closer to home.

The small-flock owner needs to consider very seriously the amount of imported wool being used by handspinners. Many small spinning/weaving shops now purchase two to three tons of handspinning wool a year from New Zealand or Australia. Much of this could be supplied by our own sheep.

The owner of the Romni Wools shop in Vancouver, B.C. says, "I would just love to buy local wool, but I can't find local fleeces that are of the standard required by handspinners." So this small shop imports 10 to 20 tons of Australian wool every year. This importing is repeated by shops all over Canada and the United States, but this market could be filled by domestic wools if the fleeces were of a comparable quality for spinning.

Spring Creek Farm in Minnesota sells its own prime fleeces to handspinners by mail but has to buy more in order to supply its demand. The farm is able to get some wool from selected local growers who will take the trouble to raise the higher quality wool required to earn the better price. But it is still necessary for the farm to import wool to fill orders. Judy Lewman of Spring Creek says, "We hope to be able to offer U.S. fleeces exclusively — but for the time being we will continue to purchase New Zealand wools whenever we're unable to locate sufficient quantities of *prime* fleeces closer to home." The emphasis on the word "prime" is most significant. She says that her prime fleeces are real "super wools," available in white and various natural colors, and are well skirted, with a minimum of 4-inch staple, as well as free of contamination from vegetable matter.

An example of the "small-scale" foreign competition is a retired couple in New Zealand who have established a thriving business by selecting the best fleeces from the shearings at local commercial sheds as they are sheared. They are marketing these to spinners in the United States, Germany, and Switzerland. In their first year, 1975, they sent only about 2,000 pounds to the United States. By 1982, this had increased to 20,527 pounds of white wool (much of this for dyeing) and 13,697 pounds of natural dark wools. Some of this was to very small weaving shops that, according to the New Zealanders, "carry only a token stock for the impulse buyer," and the rest was by mail order direct to spinners. Some packages are to guilds who send collective orders. The couple's brochure states:

The service supplying the fleeces is a personal one, these highest quality fleeces are personally selected by an experienced handspinner, and the sheep are shorn by top grade shearers. The fleeces are fully skirted of any extraneous matter and are of good staple length....New Zealand Crossbred wool from Romney, Perendale and Coopworth....recognized throughout the world as being the most suitable for handspinning. These people advertise in fiber magazines, along with other suppliers of imported wools.

While the spinners' market is a large and viable one, many growers don't take it seriously. They still think that the amount of wool used by spinners is just a drop in the bucket. The large growers can afford to take that attitude, but small-flock owners need to get the best return per sheep in order to have a profitable situation.

If you wonder about the potential market, it is estimated that there are at least 200,000 people in the United States who are engaged in spinning and/or weaving. There are many cottage industry wool enterprises that are importing large quantities of raw wool. These would be potential customers for good-quality domestic wool. In addition, there are well over 400 local and regional weaving and spinning guilds. Spinning wheels and looms are manufactured by over 50 companies in North America.

By taking woolgrowing seriously, selling at the best possible price, and taking advantage of the wool-incentive payment (page 123), you can make sheepraising profitable.

Importance of Wool Quality

Try to learn how a prime fleece should look. It is of great importance to recognize the value of prime fleece, and how good it really is, and to be able to differentiate between prime wool and good average wool. A great deal of the difference is cleanliness — lack of vegetation.

It is a waste of your best wool to send it to a wool pool, where you'll receive a price that is being paid for average quality. The fleeces you have that are obviously above average in cleanliness, color, and general attractiveness should be marketed in such a way as to obtain a price in keeping with that quality. Because factories can manufacture from a lower-quality product than that needed by handspinners, it makes sense for factories to pay only for the lowest grade that their machinery can efficiently process into the final product.

While vegetation in wool is an annoyance in factory production, it can be removed by carbonizing. The wool is treated in a 6 percent sulfuric-acid bath, dried, and baked at temperatures increasing from 180° to 200° F. The action of heat and acid on the burrs and seeds reduces most of them to carbon. The wool is then passed through rollers and shaken to remove the dust. This is followed by a sodium-carbonate bath to neutralize the acid. There is a loss of weight due to removed vegetation, as well as some loss of wool fiber during carbonization.

Handspinners who have purchased contaminated wool must remove vegetation by more tedious means. Some of the fine seeds will fall out when the wool is run through a wool picker, but the rest must be removed individually by hand. The spinner is not pleased.

Shearing

It takes a sheep a year to grow a good fleece, and it is a waste to have its value downgraded as a result of poorly managed shearing. (Read the section on shearing on pages 37-39).

If you do not shear your own sheep, you could get together with another grower to have a professional shearer do both flocks at the same time. Try together to assure that fleeces are handled in a way to make them most valuable for the handspinner.

A shearing tarp or plywood floor should be provided, of a minimum size of 5' x 5', and kept free of dirt and straw. A broom and a spring-tooth leaf rake should be standard equipment and *used*. Spinners do not want their black fleeces contaminated with white snips, or white fleeces containing dark wool or dark snips. Coarse gravel is recommended as a better ground cover in a holding area than sawdust or wood chips, which can contaminate the wool.

The shearer should understand what you want and be willing to cooperate. He (or she) should use only new oil on shearing heads, for used lubricating oil will stain the wool.

There are various opinions about the best time to shear, and it often depends on climate as well as on breeding and lambing time. In some areas, with shelter available, ewes are sheared in the fall or in winter, prior to lambing. If breeding takes place in hot weather, it is sometimes an advantage to shear prior to breeding. Shearing or tagging (cutting off locks of dung) before the fly season is helpful. Heavy manure tags on unsheared sheep can attract flies. However, if the sheep are sheared in hot weather, the inevitable nicks and cuts can also attract flies. Maggot infestation of a wound can be serious and even fatal if not discovered and treated.

In general, shearing more than once a year can be wasteful in terms of time and effort, and with most breeds it would reduce the value of the fleece for handspinning, because the wool would be shorter than the spinners want. Even with long-wool breeds, spinners like a staple length that is in keeping with the wool diameter and crimp.

If you are not shearing before lambing, tagging or crutching will eliminate the soiled fleece and let the lambs locate the udder more easily, lessening their risk of ingesting germs.

When it comes to careful shearing, it is better to have the sheep look a little ragged than to have its appearance tidied up by overlapping strokes that make second cuts, which lower the value of a spinning fleece. Fleeces should be skirted (see directions on pages 39-40), and none of the tags allowed to remain with the fleece. For spinners, you would want to remove any other parts of the fleece that are badly contaminated with grain or hay or burrs.

Paper twine is the only proper twine to use if you are tying fleeces. Twine of vegetable-fiber origin, as well as any type of synthetic or plastic twine, can contaminate fleeces, causing problems whether the fleece is to be used in handcrafts or in factory production.

Remember the competition. In Australia and New Zealand, a good handspinning fleece is expected not only to be skirted, but so clean and of such high quality that it can be easily spun without either washing or carding.

Continue to care for the wool after it is sheared and skirted. Damp fleeces should not be packed into bags, and bags should not be stored on damp cement or the dirt floor of a barn where moisture can enter the wool. Do not toss unwrapped fleeces on the top of hay bales where they can get littered with hay leaves.

Storing Wool

For long-term storage of wool (up to a year) a good procedure is to stuff the wool tightly into large paper sacks, such as double-paper feed sacks turned inside out to remove any grain. If there is bright dyed lettering on the outside of the sack, you will have to keep it right side out so that the wool is not stained. In either case, place a few moth balls on the top. Moths cannot get through the thick paper, and are discouraged by moth balls. Pack the wool tightly to minimize possible damage, for if it is loosely packed, moths can easily penetrate the entire fleece. For extra protection, you could tape the sack shut, with an identifying sample of the wool on the outside. However, wool exposed to moths *before* it is sealed could have eggs inside the bag, giving the larvae a sheltered place to multiply.

Plastic bags are not suitable for long storage of wool. Wool inside plastic sweats during any changes of temperature, creating a real possibility of combustion as well as fleece damage. Furthermore, moth balls are not recommended for use inside plastic, because the plastic may react with the moth balls or flakes to stain the wool.

If you have a good separate room or building, it could be used as a storage place for wool that you will sell right from your farm. Priscilla Blosser-Rainey of The River Farm has a separate building in which she displays all her fleeces for sale on slatted wooden shelves. Just before shearing time every year, she reduces the price on any fleeces that may be left over from the previous year. Then she cleans out her shed and sprays against moths in preparation for the new clip.

Wool Grades

There are basically about ten grades of wool produced in the United States — those listed below. (Refer to the explanation of grading systems on pages 12-14.) Each grade can be broken down into various categories according to color, length, and condition.

By contrast, there are approximately 126 different grades (or types) of wool that can be readily imported into the United States and Canada from both Australia and New Zealand. In 1981, the United States imported 19,995,000 pounds of wool

Count system	Micron system	Blood system	Crimps/inch
70s 64s	19.15-20.59 20.60-22.04	fine	15-30
62s 60s	22.05-23.49 23.50-24.94	½ blood	10-14
58s 56s	24.95-26.39 26.40-27.84	⅜ blood	8-10
54s 50s	27.85-29.29 29.30-30.99	¼ blood	5-8
48s & lower	31.00 & higher	low ¼	2-5
36s	39.7	braid	0-2

from Australia and 7,070,482 from New Zealand. In 1982, it was 20,604,150 pounds from Australia and 6,122,512 from New Zealand. This was in addition to the wool coming from Great Britain, France, and Argentina, all of which sent significant amounts.

(Actually, these figures on imports are somewhat misleading, as they do not include the small packages, 61 pounds or less, labelled "Raw Natural Greasy Wool for Handspinning and Educational Purposes" that were shipped direct to spinners.)

Wool Grading: Sorting for Handcrafters

Small-flock wool grading, when for handcraft purposes, is not really grading as the term is ordinarily used — it is selecting or sorting. By selecting out the very best and cleanest of the fleeces, you have separated out the highest quality, and can price it accordingly.

In *white* fleeces, it is difficult to predict scoured wool whiteness with any accuracy, just by looking at the greasy fleeces. However, when fleeces have been washed, they could be sorted and classified as

◆ The best white, the very whitest
◆ Creamy white, still good value
◆ Grayish white, which can be used for dyeing, blending, or quilt batts
◆ Yellow white, which can also be dyed or used in quilts or blended with other wool colors
◆ Discolored white fleeces, easier sold after dyeing

If you are selling white fleeces in the grease, you could wash a sample lock to display with each fleece, showing what it would look like after washing.

In selecting *dark* fleeces, you have more factors to consider, and you might elect to sort out the most attractive colors, or greater color variety, or longest staple, even packaging the wool in quantities of less than a whole fleece, to take advantage of color variety.

In sorting to establish the quality or desirability of a particular fleece, which in turn will be reflected in the price you ask, keep in mind the factors that are considered undesirable by spinners:

◆ Fleece with an excessive amount of vegetation
◆ Noticeable excess of second cuts
◆ Tender or weak wool (caused by poor nutrition, illness, or internal parasites in the sheep)
◆ Overly dry, weathered tips, or tippy wool (wool whose tips contain hardened grease and dirt)
◆ Musty-smelling fleece (the result of storing damp wool)
◆ Steely, brittle wool (often caused by copper deficiency)
◆ Cotty or matted fleece
◆ Dusty matted tips, which are often tender and will pull off
◆ Accumulation of grease at the tips, which often show stains even after washing
◆ Fleece length of less than 2 inches
◆ Kemp fibers, which are harsh and dye poorly, similar to head and leg wool
◆ Fleece with ticks or tick eggs, which often leave stains
◆ Urine and grass stains, or stains from dips or wormers
◆ Canary-yellow stain (caused by hot humid temperature before shearing)
◆ Excessively greasy fleece
◆ Unskirted wool with dung tags, face wool, belly or leg wool left in the fleece

Once you have sorted out the best of your fleeces, the lower quality can still sell if priced accordingly. It will be the middle-of-the-road product, for the middle price. You may well find that you can sell even the tags and skirtings if the price is right. These can be used for felting. It always helps to salvage the waste, if possible and economical. Some sheepraisers find that their children are interested in turning the tags and skirtings into income, and will take the time needed to do it. A systematic program of washing and storing the lower-quality wool can result in quite a stock of it over a period of time. When washed, such wool may still be sufficiently attractive to bring a good price for spinning or to be offered to felters. If it is machine-carded, it is made even more attractive and easier to use.

Marketing Raw Wool

There is profit in aggressively working all the angles when marketing. Imaginative promotion, interesting advertising, and stimulation of unusual uses of your product will result in busy sales.

Try selling fleeces by sheep name. Spinners can be encouraged to request the same sheep's fleece the following year if they are happy with it this year. Repeat customers are your assurance that your product is pleasing the market.

Knowing how to spin will really help in selling wool to spinners because you will understand their needs. It will also give another wool-related source of income, in case you want to sell yarn. By joining the local spinners' guild, you will be in contact with the prime prospects for fleece purchasing. Ask if you may bring some of your best fleeces to a meeting. Most small guilds have a sell-and-swap table set up after their meetings.

Have a shearing day with specials. Invite all the spinning guilds and weavers within driving distance. Let spinners choose fleeces before or after shearing. Some growers find it helps sales to allow the spinners themselves to skirt the fleeces and buy only the very best wool (at a price relative to the quality, of course). This approach could possibly sell all the choice wool that you have for the season at one time. The remaining wool could still be of a quality that is marketable to a wool-pool type market, or could be considered for washing and selling in small packages.

There is a certain small market for yarn in the grease, for knitting heavy sweaters. This yarn must be from choice wool that does not need a hot-water washing. If your wool is that

Shearing Day at Wool Findings. Because the day is well publicized, the farm sells much of its annual wool crop on this one day.

nice, you may be able to advertise it for that particular use and corner a specific market at a good price per pound. Or, if you spin, you might produce that kind of yarn and sell the yarn *or* the wool to make it, advertising them both at once.

Find uses for "waste" wool, and pursue them. For felting, weathered wools and belly wool actually work better.

Advertising may be the important key in getting your products known. If you have a large volume to sell, there are many national magazines that cater to the wool craftsperson (see "Sources"), and advertising in their classified sections would be a good investment. Buy space in at least four issues to be sure that people become familiar with your name. They may not be in the market for wool the first time they see the ad, but by the time they are, yours is a familiar name and they are more prone to buy from you. If you have only a small quantity to sell, advertise in local newspapers.

Consider selling wholesale when you have an excess of

wool. Small spinning/ weaving shops in your area could be potential outlets for wool. The smaller shops are not in a position to buy large quantities of imported wool all at one time, and should be interested in yours *if* the price and quality would allow them to sell it at a price that is competitive with the large shops that do import wool.

Contact spinners' guilds within a few nearby states (postage costs make selling close at hand more feasible) and take ads in their newsletters. These are nearly always inexpensive, and just a couple of sales would make an ad worthwhile. A series of ads ahead of shearing would be good timing. Invite the guilds to shearing, or to visit the day after shearing if shearing day sounds too hectic. This is as good as a discount if they get first choice of all your wool. Point this out.

The more you publicize your shearing day, the better attendance will be. This flyer from McFarland Romneys offers a number of attractions including give-aways, Angora rabbits, and wools from popular sheep.

Offer both washed and grease wool, but be sure you know the amount of shrinkage so that you price the washed wool realistically. Do a test on preweighed fleeces to calculate the average weight lost in washing your particular wool, and then decide on the price you will charge. You may find it is profitable to wash the dirtiest of your fleeces, as they are the ones that would be rejected otherwise.

Packaging can contribute to the attractiveness of wool. If you have a small shop at your farm, find a variety of ways to put up wool for sale. In addition to whole fleeces, try 1-pound packages, in both grease and washed wool. Have some "beginner spinner" kits that contain a pound of wool and a drop spindle, for instance. Remember to keep any plastic-packaged wool out of direct sunlight, which causes it to sweat within its package.

An upbeat attitude is always an asset to sales. Enthusiasm and product knowledge will attract customers; if they enjoy their dealings with you, they are more likely to return.

Be sure, too, to read the merchandising information in chapter 9.

Factory Wool Preferences

American mills, when asked to list the advantages of U.S. wools, could cite only availability and the necessity for use of American wool in government contracts.

For factory use, the disadvantages they listed were lack of good 60s wools, variations with the fleeces, black and colored hairs in white fleeces, excessive second cuts, black fibers from plastic twine, paint contamination, high quantities of vegetable matter, and lack of skirting.

When the wool pools of the Sonora area of Texas started a movement to put up better wools and a cleaner product, it took a few years, but factory buyers eventually began to notice the consistency of their practice and the cleanliness of their product and started paying a premium for Sonora wools. While handspinners may pay the best prices for good wool, even commercial users will pay more for better value. Buyers who are members of the American Textile Manufacturers Institute say that they would pay quite a bit more for American wools, including medium wools, if the wools were kept clean and put up without the contaminants that discount the wool price. This is of more potential concern to the large growers, but if all American wools were upgraded, everyone would benefit from it.

In conclusion, it is worth considering what Jeffrey Birnbaum wrote in the *Wall Street Journal*:

> *The raw wool of American sheep, it seems, is often full of ground-in dirt, cockleburs and a ubiquitous new invader, black plastic twine. Sheep get so gritty, in fact, that shears sometimes spark. Before World War II the U.S. produced about 500 million pounds of wool annually; today output is closer to 110 million pounds, and half of that weight is excess stuff that must be washed away.*

Preparing and Selling Washed Wool

WOOL SOLD IN THE GREASE brings its lowest return. Washing alone can make the wool more attractive, especially to those who have a hard time believing that dirty fleece can be made into beautiful yarn. It also removes the smell, which can be offensive to some. With a ram's fleece, it may take borax or washing soda to deodorize it completely.

While washing adds more value to the wool, it also results in some loss of weight in dirt and lanolin. (It is similar to the difference between selling beef on the hoof and dressed out — it sells for much more per pound after bones and waste are discarded.) You should run a test to determine the average weight lost per pound in washing, before you decide how much price differential is profitable. The loss of weight during washing could be anywhere between 10 and 50 percent of the grease weight.

There is plenty of wool available for purchasing in the grease but very little available that has been expertly washed. By washing wool, you will be offering a service that the customer may rather not perform. For example, a spinner who lives in an apartment may not wish to wash a few pounds at a time, with no good place to dry it, and take a chance on plugging the drains with wool.

Skirting

You should skirt all fleeces before washing. This will save time, as it is much simpler than trying to sort out those same parts after the fleece is washed. (*Skirting* consists of removing a strip about 3 inches wide from around the whole outside edge of the fleece: the belly wool, leg wool, neck wool, and soiled tags. The width of the discarded strip will vary, depending on the cleanliness of the fleece. See the drawing on page 39). You might set aside the skirtings and other less desirable portions for separate washing, sale, or disposal. If washed and packaged, they could be labelled for rug wool and priced accordingly. If carded, they make good felting material.

It is important to offer high quality at a fair price. Sort out what you sell into various categories. The best will sell for the highest price, like cuts of meat. You can give your wool special names for the different grades, such as Prime, Choice, and Market; or Supreme, Medium, Average, and Skirtings. What you are doing is establishing a kind of trademark. See pages 75-77 for possible categories.

Washing

In order to sell washed wool profitably, you will need to arrange an efficient washing and drying operation. Washing really requires very little investment in equipment and not much in the way of skill and experience. It is not as hard work as it might sound, especially if done as a soaking process.

The washing procedure should wash as much wool as is practical in a home situation, with as little time and mess as possible, and get the wool clean of stickiness with the minimum amount of effort. What works out well for approximately 30 pounds of wool is a hot-water-and-detergent soaking, and one rinse. The exceptions would be for Merino or Rambouillet wools, which will almost always need two washings and rinsings to remove the gumminess and the waxy tips.

Detergent is recommended because soap leaves a film on the wool unless you rinse several times, and soap does not cut the greasiness as well as detergent. Many spinners, I've found, have other favorite washing products that also produce good results: Spic and Span, Amway L.O.C., Industrial Clean, washing soda, or Orvus, a cattle shampoo. For those like me who use a powdered grocery-store detergent, it's convenient to buy it in the 42-ounce box (approximately 10 cups), about the amount needed for a 20-gallon tub, which will wash 20 to 30 pounds of wool. Sears Roebuck sells a 20-gallon portable laundry tub, and tubs can also be found in second-hand stores for reasonable prices.

Fill your large laundry tub to within about 4 inches of the top with very hot water, too hot for your hands, add 10 cups of detergent, and stir to dissolve. (Use water softener if you have hard water.) After the detergent is thoroughly dissolved, pull the fleeces apart, shaking out as much of the seeds and dirt as possible before pushing the wool down into the tub of hot wash water. (The tub is full when you cannot get any more wool into the water.) Then, using a long stick, gently poke the wool down, making sure that the detergent penetrates completely. Put the top on the tub, or lay something over it to hold in the heat, and leave the wool to soak for 2 to 4 hours. By then the water will have cooled down somewhat, and the wool can be soused and squeezed by hand several times as you remove it from the tub. (This soaking process cannot be done well with a small amount of wool as the water cools down too quickly.)

A washing machine with a spin cycle can be used for removal of the wash water and rinse water. (An old machine could be set up just for wool.) Place as much wool as the machine will hold into two mesh bags and run them through the spin cycle. (Make the mesh bags yourself.) Repeat this procedure to extract the wash water from all the soaked wool. A centrifugal extractor, built specifically for spinning water out of laundry, is the most efficient machine for water removal. These spin faster than washing machines, so they get out more water. However, do not overdo the spinning if you are using a high-speed centrifugal extractor, as too long a spin cycle is an unnecessary strain on the wool fibers. For more information on extractors, see chapter 10. A less expensive way to remove water, but much less efficient and more work, is with a wringer, either the hand-operated, clamp-on type or an old electric wringer washing machine. The tub of such a machine, with the gyrator removed, could be used to soak the wool instead of the 20-gallon laundry tub. Use of an electric wringer requires two people, one to feed the wool into the wringer, the other to keep it coming out the other side, as it has a tendency to wrap around the rollers.

Rinsing

Once the wool has been soaked and the wash water extracted, the wool is ready for rinsing. To avoid felting, which is caused by extreme changes in temperature, make sure the rinse water is about the temperature of the slightly cooled wash water, but still hot enough to take out the dissolved dirt and grease. An abrupt change of temperature, over 15 degrees, will shock the wool, resulting in a certain amount of matting or felting.

Run a tub half full of the hot water, which will be sufficient to rinse half of the washed wool. Add a bit of water softener if you are using hard water. Taking a double handful at a time, squish the wool up and down in the rinse water, squeeze the water out, and plunk the wool into a mesh bag. Fill two mesh bags and run them through the spin cycle, and repeat until you have rinsed half of the wool. Run out the dirty rinse water (it will look about as dirty as the wash water) and again fill the tub half full with clean water to rinse the rest of the washed wool. When all is rinsed (only one rinse) you can put it out on wire racks to dry. Handle the wool gently now, so as not to damage its elasticity while it is wet.

With good hot water and plenty of detergent, this washing should have removed the gumminess of the wool and left it sufficiently clean to use. There will still be some remaining dirt, dried as a powder, that will come out when the wool is being teased and carded. Keep in mind that the wool will be washed again by the handspinner after it is made into yarn, which is why it is not urgent to rinse several times to get out all the remaining dirt.

Hydrogen peroxide can be used to remove stains from the tips of white long wools. After the wool is washed, while it is still wet, the tips can be laid in a shallow glass dish and covered with peroxide. Let them stand in the peroxide as long as necessary to bleach out the stains. This would be impractical for large quantities, but is useful for small, select batches.

Drying

Drying the wool will be greatly facilitated if it can all be washed in summer weather after shearing. If this is not possible, or if you want to wash the wool as needed so that you always have a supply of both grease and washed wool to offer your customers, then you will need an adequate area for both indoor and outdoor drying racks.

In winter, wool can be dried indoors near a heat source, although a slower drying might be preferable. If drying the wool near heat, shake it out or turn it on the racks occasionally. After it's dry, allow the wool to rest in a cool place for a day, in open bags or boxes, to regain its elasticity and absorb a bit of moisture, before doing any picking or carding.

Outdoors, wool can be draped over fences, clotheslines, or porch railings, but slatted wooden racks or wire racks are more satisfactory. Stacked racks make efficient use of space and help protect against gusts of wind that could blow the wool on to the ground. These racks could be used outdoors in summer and indoors with a ventilating fan in the winter. Sachiye Jones uses an extra-large, homemade plywood fruit dryer to dry her fleeces in the winter. In the summer, when her wool is being dried on outdoor racks, the fruit dryer goes back to use with the usual fruit and vegetables.

An average wash of 30 pounds of wool would require a

drying area of about 160 square feet. This could be a 4-foot strip of chicken netting 40 feet long, or the equivalent. The netting need not be permanently framed; it can be draped on ladders or poles laid across sawhorses. This much space would allow you to lay out the wool in a suitable density for quick drying.

E. Kenneth Coltas of Ontario has designed and built a folding table/drying rack for small quantities of wool, and he has consented to let me offer his plans and directions at the end of this chapter.

Sorting

Once wool is washed, you may want to sort some of the fleeces. Dark wool can be sorted for color and packaged in 1- or 2-pound packages of a single shade. Do not sort for color prior to washing, because the colors are not as recognizable. Also, if you sort ahead of washing, it will interfere with the efficiency of large-quantity washing.

After the washed wool is dry, do a preliminary sorting while it is all spread out on the drying racks. Sorting categories could include the following:

◆ **Cleanliness.** Your cleanest wool should bring the highest price from handspinners. It should not have foreign matter such as hay seeds, twigs, bedding straw, grain, wood chips, or sawdust.

◆ **Shearing quality.** Too many second cuts (double cuts) will lower the value of the wool.

◆ **Soundness of fibers.** Weak staple caused by a sheep's illness or undernourishment makes the wool less valuable to spinners. This wool could be set aside for feltmaking.

◆ **Badly weathered tips.** These can come off in teasing and carding, and show up as lumps in handspun yarn. This kind of wool is good for feltmaking or for carding into quilt batts.

◆ **Color.** The whitest white wool, if it is free from

Wool Sorting

1. **Topknot.** *Very light, short, and inferior wool. Skirt this off.*
2. **Neck wool.** *Very light-conditioned and long-stapled wool; the folds also contain coarse, matted lumps of inferior wool. Skirt this off.*
3. **Shoulder wool.** *The best wool grown by the sheep. Sheep judges usually take the shoulder wool as a standard and see how the wool on the other portions of the sheep compares with it.*
4. **Fleece wool.** *Good, average fleece wool, usually free of vegetable matter.*
5. **Brisket wool.** *Similar to shoulder wool, but usually a little heavier condition.*
6. **Back wool.** *Inclined to be open and mushy.*
7. **Britch wool.** *Coarser wool than the other portions of the fleece and in many cases inclined to be kempy; this wool is also matted with burrs or seeds.*
8. **Arm piece.** *Very short wool surrounded by fribby edges; burrs or seeds collect heavily on this portion of the fleece. Skirt this off.*
9. **Hairy shanks.** *Hairy or kempy fibers; they can be blended with other wools or used for such articles as saddle blankets and rugs.*
10. **Stained wool.** *Wool that will not wash white, and is very heavy in condition. Skirt off.*
11. **Belly wool.** *Bulky wool, heavy in condition, and at times very burry or seedy. Skirt off.*

vegetation, will be your best-quality white, at the highest price. The creamy white can sell for less, and the discolored white at the lowest price. The latter may be labeled as dyeing wool to suggest the suitable use for it. There is not usually any justification for dyers to pay the high price of extra-white wool.

◆ *In dark wools,* the darkest blacks and good brown shades usually bring the best prices. Also, very clear gray shades, the blue-gray colors, may command a somewhat better price than the tannish grays.

◆ **Fineness and softness.** A fairly long-staple fine wool would bring a better price than a short-staple, especially if it is very clean. A long luster wool that feels soft to the touch will bring a better price than an equivalent wool that feels wiry.

◆ **Length of staple.** Most spinners prefer the maximum length of staple in the wool type they select.

Dyeing

Dyeing is an excellent option to consider in order to sell otherwise unattractive white wool. Such wool can be washed and dyed, or washed, dyed, and picked, to blend two or more colors. Packaging for sale could be in 1-pound packages of one color, or in packages of 1 or more pounds of assorted colors.

Chemical dyes are the most efficient method of dealing with substantial quantities of wool and can result in either bright and bold colors or more subtle hues. There is a very good book by Linda Knutson, *Synthetic Dyes for Natural Fibers,* listed in "Sources," that can give you all the information you need. However, considering the time involved, you will need to dye in fairly large quantities to make it profitable. It takes hardly any more time to dye 10 pounds than it does to do 1 pound.

Be sure you handle all the chemicals with caution, using a dust mask when working with powders and rubber gloves when working with liquids, and have adequate ventilation.

In theory, you should be able to charge more for dyed wool if a vegetable dye was used, but in practice that may not always be the case. If you *do* opt for vegetable dyes, it is still necessary to dye in quantity to reduce the time spent per pound of wool. *Mono-mordanting* is a great time-saver, for the wool can be washed and rinsed and go directly into the dye bath, which also contains the *mordant* (dye fixative). Separate mordanting and drying and rewetting won't be necessary. This not only cuts down on the time required for vegetable dyeing but eliminates the double-boiling of the wool that otherwise would be necessary, thus safeguarding quality and resulting in brighter colors. In my own mono-mordant dyeing, I use only one mordant combination: alum (potash alum) with cream of tartar (bitartrate of potash), both of which are ecologically safe for a farm situation and nontoxic in handling. The Center for Occupational Health in Ontario says that alum is relatively nontoxic unless consumed in large quantities, and that cream of tartar has low toxicity (although it is a laxative if consumed in large quantities). Other commonly used mordants are more dangerous: the lethal dose for an adult is 1 teaspoon of copper sulfate, 7 drops of potassium dichromate (chrome), or 1 ounce of ferrous sulfate — and these amounts would all be considerably less for children. Even vegetable dyes, particularly the mordants, must be treated with care.

There are many books on vegetable dyes in the "Sources" section, and you might want to look at them in a library or craft shop before deciding which ones to buy.

The most common color obtained from vegetable dye is yellow. Bright reds and good blues are usually from purchased cochineal and indigo. Good greens are obtained most easily by top dyeing yellow with indigo. An alternate is to add indigo "extract" to yellow dye bath.

When selling dyed wool, you will want to be able to advise your customers about colorfastness. Washfastness is fairly reliable. Sunfastness is different — you should do a fastness test. Conceal half of a small wool sample in paper and ex-pose the rest to strong sunlight for a week. Then compare the two halves to decide the degree of fastness so you know what to tell your customers.

Selling Retail

To sell retail, it is necessary to let the customers know what you have for sale, either through advertising or some other kind of promotional activity. Once you are established, word-of-mouth recommendations are your very best advertising. Your customers will probably be in the following categories:

◆ Handspinners, who will find your wool more attractive when it is clean
◆ Dyers, most of whom dye washed wool in the fleece, then card and spin it
◆ Weavers, who may want long wool locks for weaving without spinning, especially for fleece rugs
◆ Felters, whose work consumes large quantities of wool (for their use, washed *and* carded wool would be better than just washed)
◆ Less obvious users, such as ballet dancers, who use washed wool to pad the toes of their shoes

A sheepraiser who has a small building to devote to wool selling can have it organized for attractive display of wool. An ideal arrangement would be two small rooms, one for grease wool, one for washed wool. You could keep enough washed wool on hand for your customers who want it, and always wash more as needed from your supply of grease wool.

If you do not spin, you might need the advice of a spinner to know which fleeces would sell best in the grease and which you should wash. In general, it might be necessary to wash the dirtiest fleeces in order to sell them at all.

Selling Wholesale

When selling washed wool wholesale, you will be primarily selling to spinning/weaving shops. There are two ways you could sell: on consignment or outright. If on consignment, the store will take up to 40 percent of the selling price. If direct sale, that would be at least 50 percent. The store will have to charge twice what it pays per pound to make it worthwhile to stock the wool and invest in it. If you price the wool too high, it could not be marked up sufficiently to support the store overhead. Shops have a few problems in addition to pricing, connected with wool sales. They take a loss if moths infest the wool, and they take a loss if there are problems of shoplifting or bad checks. In addition, they may be left with some unsalable wool after the customers pick it over and buy the best.

Wool packaged in 1-pound bags will eliminate the problem of the best being picked out. If the wool is packaged in plastic, perforated bags will help prevent sweating, but like all plastic bags they would have to be kept out of direct sunlight. Be aware that perforated bags give no moth protection.

People buying raw wool in a shop are more likely to buy it in quantities of a pound or two, which is a good reason to make small packages. If they are interested in whole fleeces, they are more apt to seek out the sheepraiser, or order whole fleeces by mail, rather than buying in a shop.

Once you start supplying a store, it is important to maintain continuity. Arrange for a back-up supply from other sheepraisers if the store needs more wool or a greater variety than you have available.

Fleece Drying and Sorting Rack

A drying and sorting rack can be used in three ways. When fully opened, it can be used for skirting, sorting, or grading. The 1-inch mesh allows chaff and seeds to fall through. In the half-open position it serves as a drying frame for scoured or dyed fleece. The cover allows good air circulation with no wind loss. And when covered with a 72" x 31" sheet of ½-inch plywood, it converts to a useful bench for a drum carder.

The rack can be simply supported on trestles. However, collapsible steel legs are preferable. These can be purchased from most hardware or building-supply stores. The height of the rack should be about 30 inches to be comfortable for a person of average height.

BUILDING A DRYING RACK

MATERIALS FOR DRYING RACK

White pine or other wood
4 pieces for sides: 2" x 2" x 72" (1½" x 1½" dressed lumber)
4 pieces for ends: 2" x 2" x 31" (1½" x 1½" dressed lumber)
Waterproof glue
8 galvanized carriage bolts: ¼" x 2", with nuts and washers
Hinges
    1 plated butt hinge with wood screws: 3" x 3"
    2 strap hinges: 3"
Hardware cloth or any mesh that won't rust (*not* poultry netting, which
    might stretch): 4 yards of 30-inch wide cloth
Molding (sold as "doorstop" in lumber yards):34 feet of ½" x 1"
Galvanized 1-inch nails: ¼ pound

ADDITIONAL MATERIALS FOR RACK WITH FOLDING LEGS

White pine or other wood for battens, 4 pieces: 1" x 4" x 31"
Wood screws (cadmium plated)
    18 flathead: 1½" No. 8
    20 normal head: ¾" No. 10
    2 normal head: 3" No. 12
    2 normal head: 2" No. 10
Folding legs (from any hardware store)
    Jacmorr 7 514: 25" x 38½" *or*
    Waterloo: 24¾" x 28"
Hardwood round dowel or equivalent scrap strips: 8 feet of ¾-inch

Miscellaneous
2 feet of ½-inch rope
Four ½-inch washers

The finished rack with folding legs can be folded in half for storage.

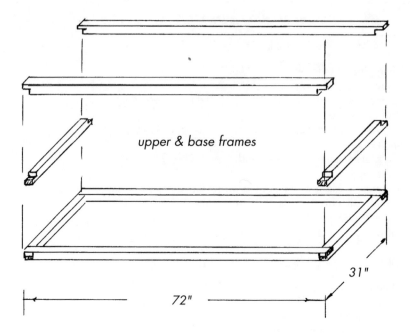

upper & base frames

72"

31"

Step 1. *Make two frames, using half-lap joints and waterproof glue. Clamp the joints, make certain the frames are square, and allow to set at room temperature overnight. Bolt each corner with a ¼" x 2" galvanized carriage bolt.*

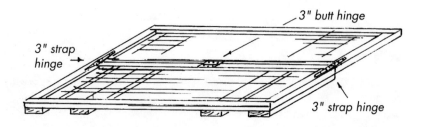

3" butt hinge

3" strap hinge

3" strap hinge

Step 2. *Hinge the two frames together with two strap hinges and the butt hinge. Next, fold the frames together, cut the hardware cloth or mesh to length with side cutters, and fasten it to the frame with a staple gun or with ½-inch staples; keep the wire fairly taut. Do not overstretch, or you will distort the frame.*

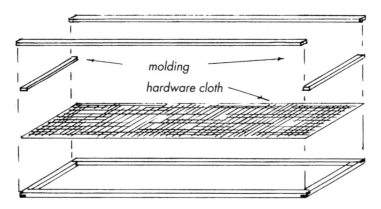

Step 3. *If you plan to use the rack with trestles, finish both frames, covering the edges of the wire with the ½" x 1" molding fastened with galvanized nails 3 to 4 inches apart.*

Building a Rack with Folding Legs

Steps 1 *and* **2**, *as above.*
Step 3, *finish only* one *frame, as above.*

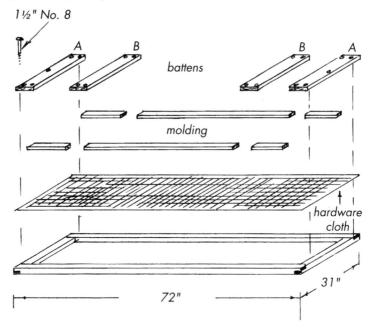

Step 4. *On the second frame, after stapling down the wire mesh, attach two A battens flush with each end, using five 1½-inch, No. 8 flathead*

wood screws in each batten. Screw a set of legs to each of these battens, using ¾-inch No. 10 wood screws. Place the legs at right angles to the frame, with the braces fully extended. Locate the B battens so that the brace brackets can be screwed to them while allowing the legs to fold flat. Screw the B battens to the frame, using four 1½-inch, No. 8 flathead wood screws for each batten. Complete the frame by nailing strips of ½" x 1" molding to cover the exposed edges of wire.

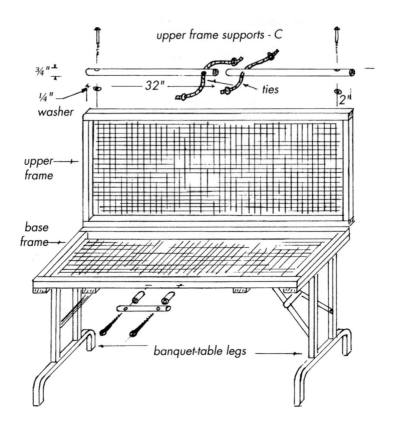

***Step 5.** When the frame is open, two auxiliary legs (upper frame supports) are needed. These are made of ¾-inch hardwood dowel. Drill a hole about 2 inches from the end of each leg to take a 2-inch No. 10 roundhead wood screw, which will serve as a pivot. The legs should be about 31 inches long overall, but it is best initially to make them somewhat longer. They can then be cut off after assembly so that the upper and base frames are level. It is a good idea to drill a ¼-inch hole about 4 inches from the bottom of each leg to take about a foot of*

¼-inch rope. When the rack is folded for storage or transport, the rope can be used to tie the whole assembly tightly together.

If the rack is to be used outdoors, it should be given a coat of suitable wood sealer and two coats of spar varnish or exterior enamel.

HANDLE DETAIL

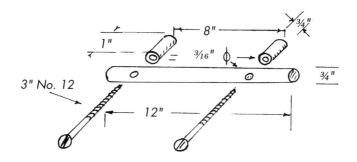

Carding as a
Cottage Industry

THE CARDING PROCESS is an important step in the wool's journey from the sheep to the finished article. And this importance offers entrepreneurs a good opportunity to set themselves up in business for a relatively small capital outlay.

Carding may be the final process done by a sheepraiser wishing to get a greater return for wool, or the initial step for the fiber artist who is preparing raw materials. It could be the principal activity of the custom carder who is also offering to scour, pick, and card wool for others. Or, it could be an element in other income-producing situations.

Basic Research

In any case, if you're thinking about carding as a business, you need to gather information ahead of time regarding outlet for your products and services. Are there any known potential customers in your area? Perhaps handspinning guilds? Where is the nearest mill or small facility offering custom carding? Does it have problems that you could overcome? Large facilities, for example, may be unable to process small quantities and therefore can't attract spinners. A mill too far away may cost too much for shipping. If there's a mill in your area, that needn't mean you can't offer carding; two (or more) wool processing plants can successfully operate in the same area if they're serving different types of customers. Also, investigate your zoning regulations. Plan your work space. Do you have some mechanical aptitude or interest, or know someone who has? Do you have access to quantities of wool for resale? Subscribe to fiber publications for information on how other businesses are operating. Consider mail order to reach more customers. Evaluate the effect your sales would have on your wool-incentive income (for further information, see pages 123-24).

Facilities

For a well-rounded business that offers washing, picking, and carding services, consider, as a minimum, space equal to three bedrooms of a house. Three spaces. One would be needed just for storage, including receiving and shipping. You can have outdoor washing facilities and outdoor racks for drying in the summer, but you still need indoor ones for bad weather. Shelves are necessary for storing identified wool orders, and these can be in the drying room.

Your picking and carding can be done in the same area if you are using a hand-operated wool picker. The picker should be bolted onto a solid, 2-foot-wide table. A powered picker would take more space, an area about 5' by 12', to give you comfortable working room. The powered Cottage Industry carder is 30 inches wide and 84 inches long, including the roving elevator. You would need a minimum of 2 feet of working space on each side of the machine.

While in the early stages, you can get away with cramped quarters, but think ahead for expansion. Indulge in a little advance planning.

Get set up to do an efficient job of wool washing and drying. To be machine carded, the wool *must* be free of grease, and the best person to clean it is the one who is going to do the carding. If the customer is to wash it, send washing in-

The author with a carded wool batt similar to those used in quilts. Such batts can provide entry into a new market.

structions ahead of time, or the customer may think the wool should be washed in cool water to leave in the lanolin. Insist on offering a rewashing service if needed, for an additional fee.

Be prepared to turn down unsuitable wool. Poor material, especially heavily contaminated wools, can damage your equipment. Heavy burrs will bend carding-cloth teeth.

Wool can be carded into either a *batt* or *roving*. A batt is a mass of fibers about 4 inches thick that comes off the carder in a single wide strip; roving is carded wool in a thin, continuous strip. Roving requires higher-quality wool than is necessary for batts. Most home-carding facilities offer their customers the choice of having their wool carded into batts or into roving, but reserve the right to make the final choice, depending on the quality of the wool that is sent for carding (see pages 96-98).

Advantages of Versatility

Diversification is good business, and a wide variety of products or services can enhance your profits. If you sell wool that has been washed, picked, and carded, and even sell handspun and products made from it, you can attract more customers by offering many products. Carding helps make that possible.

Quilt batts, either as loose carded batts, or encased in muslin, are a means of reaching another market. Sheepraisers can have their best wool carded for handspinners, and the lower-quality wool will still be suitable, when well washed and carded into batts, for quilts or feltmaking.

Pricing

It is easier to justify the cost of washing, picking, and carding if you itemize each service separately on your price list. A lump sum quoted for all of the services may sound expensive, but if they are broken down into separate charges, the customer is aware of the amount of work being purchased.

The customer will bear the cost of postage on mail-order shipping, but you will need to provide the packaging — either purchased or scrounged boxes or the customer's own shipping container, which you saved for returning.

Selecting Fleece for Processing

Wool defects such as stained fleece or uneven quality do not just disappear with washing and carding, although processing may make some of them either less noticeable or less of a problem for the spinner. Many factors have a bearing on the ease of carding and the quality of the batt or roving produced. In general, you would do well to avoid the following:

◆ *Fleece with an excessive amount of vegetation.* Foreign matter can become imbedded in the carding teeth as well as interfere with the carding action, resulting in an unsatisfactory product. Contaminated wool requires added labor.

◆ *Noticeable excess of second cuts.* Fortunately, many second cuts can be shaken out of a fleece *if* it has not been compressed and stored too long. Second cuts will show up as neps or little lumps in the batt or roving.

◆ *Tender wool,* in which the wool staple can actually be pulled apart. This wool suffers severe damage in both picking and carding.

◆ *Tippy wool,* which has overly dry, weathered tips. Some

tips will come off in picking and even more in carding, making almost the equivalent of second cuts. Noticeably dusty tips may indicate weathering and future breakage during carding.

◆ *Musty-smelling fleece,* which is the result of shearing wet sheep or of wool becoming damp during storage. This musty smell is difficult to remove.

◆ *Steely wool,* which is a brittleness often caused by a copper or zinc deficiency in the diet of the sheep.

◆ *Cotty wool,* matted or felted in the fleece. Locks that are felted together can be opened during hand picking or motorized picking but with some damage to the fleece.

◆ *Short wool* (less than 2 inches). Although it is not objectionable to all spinners and has some usefulness, short wool can cause difficulties in machine carding. A staple length of less than 2 inches does not get worked properly by the carder.

◆ *Stained fleece,* with stains that will not wash out. Stains reduce the value, unless the wool is to be used for a purpose where stains can add to the effect.

◆ *Wools in which the crimp is not in keeping with fiber length.* This indicates an uneven quality in the fleece, or is the result of shearing twice a year.

To get a premium price when selling washed and carded wool, you need to recognize your choicest wool in order to make the most you can on it. Wool that is less desirable, from a spinner's viewpoint, can still be sold for other uses, or for commercial use at the going price for local wool.

Exceptionally fine wool is the most difficult to handle during both picking and carding. Fine-wool fleeces, such as Merino and Rambouillet, are always very greasy and are hard to get completely clean. If the wool is short and/or the least bit waxy or sticky, it is difficult to do a good job of carding. Fibers must slide past each other during the carding process, and gumminess inhibits this action.

Effects of Processing

Although the fineness and the crimp of the wool are relatively unaffected by your processing, the following can be affected:

◆ Grease content of the wool
◆ Moisture content
◆ Felting and matting
◆ Tensile strength
◆ Length of fibers
◆ Elasticity
◆ Luster
◆ Color
◆ Softness

Compared to factory-processed wool, wool processed at home shows minimal adverse effects and, in many instances, these can be avoided entirely. Your wool will not be getting the harsh treatment of intensive scouring and carbonizing that many commercial plants do in order to remove foreign matter. In carbonizing, wool is saturated with a mineral acid (usually sulfuric acid) and dried. It is then put through a baking machine, where the sulfuric acid and high heat act to convert the impurities into easily crumbled hydrocellulose, which can then be removed mechanically.

Your customers will be interested in knowing how gently you treat the wool during processing, so be sure to tell them!

Avoiding Neps

Neps are tiny bunches of tangled fibers. Although they are produced during carding, the cause is usually the degree of entanglement of the wool as it is fed into the carder. After carding they can easily be seen as dense areas or spots when a thin web of carded wool is held up to the light. When wool is attenuated during spinning, they are like small whorls of fibers with a pronounced core. Individual nep fibers, if untangled and measured individually, are always much shorter than the average length of the fiber being carded. This does not mean that the naturally short fibers of a fleece are more prone to snarling, but that the nep fibers probably suffered breakage after snarling, when forcibly pulled apart in carding.

Unwashed wool itself has no real neps as such, so the challenge is to get it from its unwashed state to a clean carded condition without causing neps. Neps can be prevented, in part, by

◆ *Careful washing of the fleece* (see washing instructions, chapter 5). Do not rub the wool or unduly wring or spin it, and do not run water directly onto the wool.

◆ *Thorough washing with sufficient detergent* so that the wool is not the least sticky or tacky. If it is, the fibers will not slip past each other as smoothly as they must in order to be carded properly.

◆ *Careful teasing or picking* prior to machine carding.

◆ *Adding carding-and-spinning oil* (see "Sources") if the wool seems unusually dry or prone to nep production. The addition of both oil and moisture prior to carding will have the effect of increasing fiber elasticity and flexibility while lowering breakage, as well as lubricating some of the existing tangles so they will pull free.

◆ *Allowing a resting period* between washing, picking, and carding. Fibers will regain elasticity if allowed to rest, and will be less prone to neps and other breakage.

◆ *Avoiding wool that has excessive vegetation,* which interferes with proper carding.

Quality Control

Upon receipt of a customer's wool, and before picking and carding, take a few sample locks from different parts of the fleece to check the staple length and to look for possible tenderness of the fibers or excess vegetation. See if the fleece has been adequately skirted. If it has been washed, inspect to determine if it has been washed properly to make it free of stickiness.

When wool is short, it should be made into batts, not into roving. If it is both short and fine, feed the carding machine very lightly.

When wool shows evidence of tenderness or broken fibers, put a small sample batch through the picker and examine it to make sure the staple is not being broken. The level of tenderness can vary; some tender wools can be processed without unduly affecting the end product, while other weaker wools will come apart so badly that they lower the quality of the batt, showing up as neps and lumpy texture. If the wool does appear to be overly tender, advise the customer, because you will be processing a fleece that breaks into short fibers due to the tenderness, resulting in an unsatisfactory batt. Your customer may not want to spend the money to process an inferior fleece.

It is important that all the gumminess be washed out of the fleece; otherwise the machinery will tend to roll it up rather than card it, leaving little rolled neps in the wool. If you accept sticky wool and do not rewash it, the customer will complain about the quality of the carding. The wool will also deposit gumminess on the carder's flycomb, making it necessary to clean the flycomb teeth.

Wool that has been harshly scoured, or was washed six or more months prior to the time you receive it, may appear overly dry and brittle and would benefit from a very light application of a carding-and-spinning oil that mixes with water to form a water-soluble emulsion for spraying onto the wool the day prior to picking and carding (see "Sources"). Oil makes the wool spin more readily, and washes out of the finished yarn easily. When used sparingly, it is not detectable in the carded wool. A better effect can often be obtained by using a fine misting of warm water containing about 20 to 30 percent Downy fabric softener. This acts as an anti-static agent and is a great wool conditioner for carding.

Actually, oil, moisture, and heat are of great benefit in

carding, making the wool soft and flexible so that the fibers slip easily against each other. Moisture alone produces the same effect, in a lesser degree. Combine this with a 70° F. carding room for maximum results. If it is necessary to work in an unheated room, put a heat lamp over the infeed tray — it will help considerably.

Wool should have a short resting period between washing and picking, and again between picking and carding, to allow it to regain its normal elasticity and to minimize fiber breakage.

Because you want to be selective about the wool that you accept for carding, but don't want to offend prospective customers by rejecting the wool they send, it is a good idea to have an information sheet describing the process of preparation and the process of carding.

Explain why badly contaminated wool could damage the carder and cannot be accepted for carding, and why poor wool cannot be made into roving. Tell customers why gummy wools do not card well and must be rewashed. This will allow you to reject wool that does not come up to your minimum standards. Also include a price list for washing, rewashing if the customer has not done a thorough job, picking, and carding into batts or roving. Include your washing instructions for customers who want to do their own washing.

Wool Picking

Picking is an essential part of the correct procedure in preparing wool for carding. In order to get the best performance from your carder, the washed wool (see washing instructions, pages 71-74) must be well opened, with all tangles removed. Lumpy or felted locks do not card well, either in a table top drum carder or in the Cottage Industry carder. They produce an inferior batt and could possibly damage the machine's carding teeth.

Mechanical picking replaces the laborious task of hand separating and opening the locks prior to carding. A table-top picker (see pages 139-41) speeds up this important process and removes much of the dust and fine seeds. In some cases, wool can be spun right from the picked condition. Mohair, as an example, can often be sold as washed-and-picked, ready for spinning.

As business grows and time is at a premium, consider a power-driven rotary picker. This more than quadruples the volume picked per hour, and with less effort. The power-picked product is more fluffy and lofty, due to the controlled airflow combined with the rotary picking action (see chapter 10).

During the picking process, you have a good chance to toss out foreign matter, second cuts, and any locks that are badly contaminated with vegetation and could lower the quality of the product. It is better to discard contaminated clumps rather than retain them. The more extraneous material removed in the initial stages, the better. You will be surprised how quickly you can clean up a batch of wool during picking and carding.

After picking, check the wool for second cuts. These show up plainly as small, solid lumps of wool against the longer fibers of the fluffed-up mass. They are easy to identify and should be removed. It takes only a few second cuts to reduce the quality of the entire lot of wool.

Carding

Until recently, the only way the home spinner could process wool was with hand cards, which are very slow and hard on the hands. With the advent of the table-top drum carder, this process was speeded up, allowing more time for spinning. Some small cottage industries may start with a drum carder, processing about a pound an hour, but as their demand grows, this proves inadequate.

The Cottage Industry carder, designed specifically for hand spinning wools, will process from 8 to 12 pounds per hour, making carding as a cottage industry a reality. It will produce batts of six-foot length, which can be removed while the machine is running, and the machine can be readily converted to roving production. The charge for producing batts can be lower than the charge for producing roving, and many people prefer batts — they are more convenient to ship and easier to store, while being just as easy to spin. Batts are also in demand for making comforters and felt. Any wool that is not absolutely prime will sell better in a batt.

When you are carding, lay out the wool on the infeed tray of the machine and look for dried manure that may have been left in the washed wool, or hard burrs, seeds, and grain that could damage the carder. If you are feeding the wool lightly, there is time as you work to see and remove some of the snips and second cuts that would lower the quality of the finished product. These second cuts, shorter snips, and inferior wools could be tossed into a small box beside the infeed tray to return to your customer. When these constitute a sizable percentage of the wool weight, you will not want to throw them away because the customer will wonder why there was such a loss of weight. Mention to the customer that while you did not remove all the snips, if wool in the future were carefully sheared and/or well skirted, the carded product would be improved.

Roving Production

For producing roving on the Cottage Industry carder, it is suggested that you select only the best wools, clean of excess contamination, well washed, picked, and with long or medium-long fibers. Otherwise, the following problems may be encountered:

◆ Short-staple wool will not hold together well as the roving is being produced, causing web or roving breakage.
◆ Unpicked wool will not card evenly for a roving of consistent diameter.
◆ Poor-quality wool will result in a lumpy and unattractive roving.
◆ Excess vegetation will interfere with the carding process, preventing the even draw of the fibers and resulting in a lumpy roving.

Wool should be free of stickiness (see washing instructions, pages 71-74). Any gumminess will make the wool adhere to the flycomb, creating a bottleneck ahead of the roving orifice. It will also cause excessive fiber breakage throughout the machine. Lower-quality wool, if washed clean, can be processed into batts, rather than roving, to be used for spinning rug yarn, or for quilt batts or felting.

The size of the roving will be controlled by the operator's rate of wool infeed. Fine wools can be made into roving if they are over 2½-inch staple and very clean; however, they should be fed sparingly for the best possible carding result.

Two-color or three-color rovings are a way to utilize otherwise uninteresting colors. A great amount of middle gray occurs with dark sheep when you have an overabundance of six- to eight-year-old ewes — good mothers with drab fleeces. This gray can be combined with another color (lighter or darker) in a roving, making an attractive yarn when spun. Another wool that benefits from being part of a two-color roving is off-color white. By sorting out the very best of your white to sell at a premium price, you are left

An uninteresting off-white wool, when carded together with two other natural shades, makes an attractive three-color roving.

with a lot of second-quality color. The grayed white makes a good roving when combined with dark gray or with black. Yellowed white also combines well for a two-color roving, with tan or brown. Dyed wools are exciting in two-color and three-color combinations.

Carding Dyed Wool

Dyeing, as I've already mentioned, is a good way to sell otherwise undesirable white or pale wool. Such wool can be sold as washed, dyed, and picked as a blend of two or more colors, or it can be completely processed into carded wool (see section on dyeing, pages 77-78). When two or more colors are carded, they can be done as roving, which comes out in ribbons of color, or as rainbow batts in layers of color. At a recent Black Sheep Gathering in Oregon, a booth selling spinning supplies did the majority of its sales in these dyed rainbow batts.

Whether you use chemical dyes or vegetable dyes may depend on the quantity of wool that you intend to dye, the availability of dyestuffs that you can gather locally, or the demand of your market.

At first glance, chemical dyes seem more expensive than plant gathering, although even with plant dyes you still need to buy mordants and supplies to obtain special shades. However, chemical dyes save time over dye gathering and produce far greater color possibilities, more easily duplicated colors, and some saving in dyeing time. "Sources" lists addresses of suppliers of dyes and dye books.

Wool Blending

For two or more wools to be completely integrated, they should be blended during picking. Wool can be blended for color or texture, or to obtain a larger quantity than available in any one fleece. If you have call for more pale-gray shades and fewer medium, then white can be blended into the medium gray to make a lighter shade. Short lamb's wool can be successfully added, a small amount at a time, into batches of longer wool during picking, to soften the resulting blend.

The powered wool picker (see pages 141-42) does an excellent job of blending fibers. Different lots of dyed wool can be mixed together on the picker to obtain a larger quantity if needed. To get an even blend, the different materials (either different colors or different fibers) are laid together on the infeed conveyor and thoroughly mixed as they are picked. The air currents completely mix them into an entirely new end product that is often vastly superior both in color and texture to its components. No further blending will be necessary when feeding this mixture into the carding machine.

You will find that materials combined during carding give a mottled effect.

Exotic Fiber Blends

In the last few years, the big news in the fiber world has been the fast-growing interest in exotic fibers and wool/exotic blends, and the most popular supplies are color blends and fiber blends.

As you get more skillful in the use of a Cottage Industry carder, you will probably wish to experiment with the unusual and more expensive fiber combinations. It is important to maintain a clean, well-tuned machine that will not contaminate the expensive fibers with seeds and dirt that have been picked up from previously carded, low-quality wool. This puts more emphasis on the necessity to be quite selective in what you accept, or to do much more thorough hand preparation, even on marginal wools, to protect your machine.

Blending unusual or exotic fibers with wool is a good way to enhance the attractiveness and salability of the wool. Blending increases the value of the materials and earns a better price for the blend than its components would bring individually. Silk and wool together, for instance, may sell for more than the value of the silk, which is, of course, the more costly of the two fibers. Mixing of the fibers in the powered picker can be more thorough than could be done by hand.

Blends are often superior in unexpected ways, such as the

The Jumbus Exotica has speed controls on the infeed belt as well as on the infeed drums, so the complete infeed section may be slowed down for difficult fibers and blends (shown with safety guards removed).

added ease of spinning a silk/wool/mohair blend over spinning either pure silk or mohair. Blending is not unlike a crossbreeding program, where the resultant hybrid vigor of the progeny may surpass the best qualities of the parents' breeds.

The new Jumbo Cottage Industry Carder for Exotics can successfully process alpaca, mohair/wool, silk/wool, silk/cotton, pure Angora bunny, and bunny blends. Experiment with color blending, and spin samples to see which of the proportion/color mixes are suitable. For weaving, take half of the blend and spin it right from the picker for a tweedy and textured weft yarn, then card up the rest of the blend for spinning into a more uniform warp yarn.

Another method of fiber blending is that done on the infeed tray, or on the moving infeed belt of the Jumbus Exotica, the top-of-the-line carder. When working with more than two different fibers, it may give more control if one of the fibers has been precarded and then fed along with other fibers that have only been picked.

Processing for Shares

If you have call for more processed wool than you can supply, consider carding on shares. This could work as washing-and-carding for half of the wool involved, or carding only, for a third of the wool that you process. Thus, for your labor you would be obtaining materials that you could sell or use in your own products if you spin, knit, or weave.

If someone else is going to be doing the washing, make sure it is done in accordance with your washing instructions.

Recarding Quilt Batts

From time to time you will be asked to recard old quilt batts. This sounds reasonable — until you try. The labor and frustration will far outweigh any price that could be charged. The wool is likely to be short, as well as matted and dead. It will not card at all well and should simply be returned to the customer. Even if you make a fifty-fifty mix with new wool, the result will not please. The best solution: offer new quilt batts at a lower price than the cost of recarding old quilt batts. The customer will be far happier, and you will avoid the impossible task of recarding short, matted wool. If the original wool is of sentimental value, the customer can use it to stuff a pillow.

Storage Space

Space must be organized for wool storage in order to separate the washed wool from the unwashed, and one customer's wool from another's. Your own unwashed fleeces could go on slatted shelves, unwrapped, so you can see the general color and grade of the wool. Washed white fleeces can be stored in sorting bins, sorted for fiber type and/or whiteness. Don't forget, when you empty a bin or shelf, to spray it with moth repellent before restocking. Commercial electric bug-killer lights are effective in controlling moths. While relatively expensive, they keep a whole area protected by killing the flying insects. Mouse damage can best be controlled by a resident cat.

Safety

Safety is an important factor where there is machinery. Do not take short cuts — do it the safe way. Observe all the safety precautions listed in the equipment manual, and be sure to

◆ Wear a particle-dust mask when working with dusty wool.
◆ See that seeds and dust do not pile up around the carding machine motor.
◆ Wear snug clothes and pin up long hair.
◆ Have safety lockouts on operating switches.
◆ Disconnect the power before cleaning or working on the machine.
◆ Have "No Smoking" signs, and enforce them.
◆ Have a first-aid kit available.

Income-Producing Angles

THE SECURITY OFFERED by a cottage industry can be in direct relationship to how broad its base is. The more things you have working for you, the easier it is for you to weather any decline in one branch of your enterprise. A broad-based business may require the time and skills of more than one person, so a family effort may be necessary for a greater guarantee of success.

Sheep owners can increase their total income by selling breeding stock, meat, raw wool, washed wool, processed wool, yarn, finished products, and, if possible, their own unique specialty items. It helps to capitalize on any contacts you have already from some previous business or hobby, and to develop a wide variety of wool-related products. Some sheepraisers are also dealers for allied items such as specialized fencing; some are retailing sheepcovers; and others are selling books and equipment.

I know of several husband-and-wife businesses that combine two interests, only slightly related. What comes to mind in particular are several home businesses called "Wool and Wood" that buy books from me for resale. The husband does the woodworking, mostly spinning and weaving tools, and the wife is engaged in wool-related activities. And a shop

PHOTOGRAPH BY STEPHEN O. MUSKIE

Deborah Ann Abbott, modeling a one-of-a-kind ensemble: a vest and skirt lined with silk and trimmed with natural black/gray sheepskin. Her Aurora Designs, in Keene, New Hampshire, proves the value of unique clothing: she has built a substantial business out of designing handwoven clothing (and been featured in Vogue, Fiberarts, *and other national publications). She and her husband own 200 sheep that supply wool for the handloomed fabric she sells from her showroom at 49 St. James St. in Keene, and through her catalog.*

called "A Weaver and a Potter" is doing a good business in both crafts. It is of advantage to advertise both kinds of products at once any time you advertise, partly for the economic advantage, and also to capture the interest of new customers.

Handspun Yarn

A wool seller who also knows how to spin has an obvious advantage when selling wool to handspinners. By being able to talk the language of spinners, by knowing their needs and preferences, it will be easier for you to please them, and happy customers are usually repeat customers. Joining a spinning guild will give a way of contacting wool users, and this should provide good customers unless another member of the guild has better wool for sale. Knowing how to spin well is better than just knowing how to spin; you can give lessons and thereby create a new crop of spinners who are automatically wool users. Some growers, in fact, give free lessons, charging only a materials fee for the wool used. Students will buy fleece to take home to spin and many become steady customers.

To sell handspun yarn you will need to offer sample cards, either separate cards for weavers (more textured yarn) and for knitters, or one card for both. Charge enough for the sample cards to make it worth your while to make them. You will be using up yarn and time, and paying for envelopes, printed price lists, and stamps.

Spinning your own wool also gives you a way to use up wool that is passed over by others. You can utilize many of the skirtings, for instance, if they are well washed and picked, by spinning a highly textured yarn to be sold for making rugs or wall hangings (or for use in your own weaving). Having learned to spin, and having handspun yarn for sale, you will have one more type of sheep-related income.

Using Handspun Imaginatively

I am still amazed at the large number of people who are earning a substantial part of their living selling yarn. I know that some people believe it is not possible to make a living *only* by spinning. While it is possible, it does sound monotonous. The fact of the matter is that few of us want to do nothing but sit and spin all day. It is much more rewarding to have a variety of things to do. In addition to spinning yarn, developing a product made from that handspun — a knitted or crocheted or woven article — is both profitable and fun. In a way, each will help sell the other; people may either buy the finished article or be prompted to buy the yarn to make it themselves.

Combining two different skills in one product is a way of creating a more distinctive effect. Obvious examples are crocheted edging on a woven vest or coat, a crocheted edging on a knitted sweater, or a macramé finish on a woven hanging. A little more unusual is a combination of felting with knitting or weaving, felt with soft leather, or felt with Ultrasuede.

One combination of yarn and felting is mittens knitted

with handspun yarn with cozy felted insides. The process is quite simple: ordinary knitting with a slender strip of carded unspun wool carried along on the inside and bound into the stitches as you knit. When the mittens are done, turn them inside out. With a thick soap mixture, rub them until they are lightly felted. It makes a most impressive effect, with a small amount of work.

Selling at Fairs

One good way to start selling your handspun yarn or finished products is at arts and crafts fairs. These are often seasonal, two- or three-day weekend affairs that charge entry fees for space and collect from 20 to 40 percent in commissions on sales. With most of these there is advance screening of entrants. Each person sets up a display and tends the booth for the hours of the fair.

If you have attended any of these, you will know how much depends on how things are displayed. Avoid confusion in your display — it can tire the customer to look at it. Too elaborate a display is also a mistake, since it appeals only to the aesthetic nature rather than to the desire to buy, and will draw more comments than sales. Offering more than one kind of wool product can enhance sales; combinations might be yarn and carded wool, or yarn and knitted garments, or yarn and felt. Wherever you display your wares, be sure that everything is plainly priced. Even if you are selling retail, be prepared in advance for wholesale inquiries, and have it clear in your mind whether you wish to deal with wholesalers at the kind of prices they would find acceptable. In taking orders for future delivery, be cautious about promising delivery dates; make sure you allow yourself ample time. Better to surprise your customers by being early than to be late because you were trying to please them by promising quicker delivery than you could fulfill.

For more on craft shows see pages 129-31 in chapter 9, as well as other merchandising information in that chapter.

Instructions to Customers Buying Handspun

Whether you're selling at fairs, at a shop, or by mail, customers should be provided with washing instructions and told if the yarn is preshrunk. Anyone selling handspun yarn to knitters should also be able to advise the customer about what size knitting needles to use with the yarn; otherwise the knitter may use needles that are too small. This could cause a sweater to be unnecessarily harsh, and also result in an insufficient quantity of yarn with which to finish the sweater, as smaller needles use more yarn. Using too-small needles seems to be a common mistake among people knitting with handspun for the first time. Since it is a unique material, customers must be advised how to use the handspun that you sell them. This means that *you* must know how. Some spinners develop their own line of patterns to go with their yarn and give them out with yarn orders.

Business tactics for selling yarn both wholesale and retail are detailed in *The Handspinner's Guide to Selling* (see "Sources").

Knitting from Handspun

Knitting is another way to enlarge your income by having a variety of merchandise. If you are an expert knitter, you may want to make one-of-a-kind sweaters, or custom-knit them to order. However, because of the time involved in both spinning and knitting, the same person may not wish to do both, or may not be equally proficient in both.

There are many small items that can be made from handspun that do not require as much time and skill as a sweater. Any time you are selling at a craft fair or outdoor street fair, you will find a more ready market for affordable small items than for larger and more expensive garments.

Spinners of unusual textured yarns, especially from dyed fleece, can often find retail shops or boutiques that are interested in selling their handknit sweaters. When knit with needles sufficiently large to result in soft sweaters, and done in simple

Alice Stough and her daughter, modeling handknit sweaters that are among the variety of products from Alice in Wonderland. Finding a number of ways to convert wool to income is one of the secrets of success in a wool-based cottage industry.

classic styles, handknit sweaters are in demand by the kind of shops that get high prices for exclusive clothing.

Knitting Machines

In the past ten years, knitting-machine owners have discovered the unique charm of handspun yarn, and spinners have found that there are a number of knitting-machine brands that do very well with handspun. There was a time when handspun had to be heavy and textured in order to sell, and that type of yarn was not easily used on a machine. Now, the most popular handspun is fine and evenly spun, in two-, three-, and even four-ply, and is easier to work with and more attractive than commercial yarn. Before investing in a knitting machine, be sure to try out your own handspun yarn on it, and investigate several different brands. An experienced knitter can use the machine for the bulk of the knitting, and do a hand finishing in order to produce a truly unique garment.

Knitting from Fleece

A sheepraiser who does not spin can knit with unspun wool. The preparation of the wool is tedious, but in the long run it is not too lengthy when you consider that the process makes it possible to omit the picking-carding-spinning sequence.

Using long-staple wool, 4 to 5 inches long, make bundles of wool staples about 3 or 4 inches in diameter. Secure these wool bundles together by tying them firmly (but not too tight) with strips cut from old nylon pantyhose. Soak the bundles in hot water and detergent for about an hour. Spin out the wash water by placing the fiber bundles in two mesh bags or two pillowcases and using the spin cycle of your washer. Then rinse the bundles gently in water about the same temperature as the washing water was when you removed the bundles. Put the bundles on a rack to dry; remove the ties when the wool is placed on the rack.

When dry, this wool can be knitted by gently pulling wool fibers out of the washed wool into a continuous strand. The wool will stay in fairly undisturbed condition if you have handled it carefully.

Australian Locker-Hooking with Unspun Wool

Locker-hooking is a technique that is fairly new to the U.S. and Canada. Loops of unspun wool are held in place on rug canvas by a hidden "locking" yarn. The only specialized equipment needed to do this is a locker-hooking needle, which is included with an excellent book, *Australian Locker Hooking* (see "Sources").

Rugs are the obvious product of this technique, but the work can be done on any size of needlepoint or rug canvas or other softer-mesh material to produce garments, jacket linings, pillows or smaller articles. The book has good photographs and drawings.

Weaving from Handspun

Weaving is another way to turn your handspun wool yarn into greater income per pound of wool. This is especially important if your production of wool is low and cannot be expanded due to limited pasture. Given a restricted amount of your own wool, you would need to purchase additional wool if your

The author has years of experience in growing, processing, and spinning her own wool, which she then weaves and sells as finished products or as products to be finished by shopowners.

objective was a high-volume, low-priced product. If, on the other hand, you go for a low-volume, high-priced article such as something handspun and handwoven, and are successful in making and selling it, you would realize more income from the same amount of wool used. More time and work, less wool, more money.

Before buying a loom, learn to weave. If possible, take a class where floor looms are used, to get an idea of the brand or size of loom you might want. For serious weaving, even as a hobby, you should get a floor loom. Table looms make the work go so much slower that it can be discouraging, as well as difficult to really produce. While table looms in a class will only constitute an introduction to weaving, they are still better than nothing, and you will get the idea of the weaving process and know some of its various possibilities.

If space or finances make a floor loom out of the question, you can still make salable articles on a frame loom such as a simple tapestry frame, which is inexpensive. There are a number of good books on tapestry weaving including *The Guide to Successful Tapestry Weaving* by Nancy Harvey (see "Sources"). In making tapestries that would be used as wall hangings, you would be in competition with paintings, prints, and photographs for your customers' wall space. But weavings on a frame loom or a tapestry loom can be used to make other objects that will sell well, such as purses, tote bags, rugs, and pillows. These weavings can also be incorporated in garments that are partly knitted.

Triangular frame looms can be used to make shawls, and inkle looms, which are inexpensive, can be used to weave belts, decorative borders, and even strips that can be sewn together to make larger articles.

Any previous experience or interest you have in related subjects, such as textiles, garment design, or tailoring, can be of advantage when you start weaving. It takes more than training in the technical aspects of weaving to be able to turn out yardage or clothing with a special flair or fashion sense — a well-developed color or design instinct is also needed.

Woven yardage can be sold to shops, and some of these will have a tailor make it up skillfully, and then sell the finished garment. I have seen advertisements in both *Fiberarts* and *The Crafts Report* for shops that were seeking handwoven yardage to purchase. I have woven ponchos for a shop, weaving only the poncho square, which I then fringed on all sides. The shop owner had her tailor do a velvet-lined neck opening. If a weaver lacks sewing expertise, the garments may not meet the customers' expectations. One puckered seam or imperfect place in a lining can lose a sale.

Woven rugs and upholstery fabrics can best be marketed through a shop or an interior decorator. The professionals are able to command better prices because of established reputations and markets.

Tanned Pelts

It is debatable whether sheepskin pelts are a profitable item, because of the competition from imported pelts. However, even if you cannot equal the price, a few pelts offered in addition to your other products may sell well. Dark, undyed pelts have a special appeal. A unique *product* made from tanned pelts may have no competition.

Depending on the type of product you want to make from tanned pelts, you may need them to be machine washable (glutaraldehyde tanned). The materials needed for the home tanning of washable pelts are expensive to buy, but commercial tanning of washable pelts is not much higher than if they are not washable.

A great variety of things can be made from tanned pelts. Handmade slippers with the shearling wool inside could compete with commercial slippers just by being more unusual — a specialty item with more style. Other items are better if made from pelts that have longer wool.

Pelts can be trimmed to crib size for blankets; made into little coats and vests for children, woolly toys, hot-water-bottle covers, bicycle-seat covers; cut into pieces and made into couch throws with the pieces crocheted together; or even cut into strips and woven, perhaps with scraps from other projects. While car-seat covers made from tanned shearling (and even imitation pelts) are available as commercial products, they look mass-produced (which they are) and are not as distinctive as seat covers made from really individual pelts. Personally, I think that tanned pelts simply laid across a car seat are even better, since they can easily be shaken out as necessary. Pelts can be sold as bedroom rugs, bathroom rugs, invalids' bed pads, or chair covers. You don't have to be an invalid to enjoy a pelt as a chair or bench cover. Cats love them, too, and cats have very discerning taste. Odds and ends, if you cut up shearlings to make other products, can be made into woolly insoles that are luxurious inside boots. A pile insole at one time was commercially made of 50 percent wool and 50 percent synthetic, on a woven base. Recently, it was available as only 25 percent wool and 75 percent synthetic, but the pile mashed down in just a few wearings, not having the "bounce" of wool. It would be easy to compete with that product by selling real wool-shearling insoles.

When a lamb or mature sheep is going to the slaughter house, look at it and decide what would be the best use of the skin. You could

◆ Shear the fleece for use as wool, then have the skin tanned as leather.

◆ Shear the fleece, then wait four to six weeks before

slaughter, and have the skin tanned as shearling.

◆ In the case of short lamb's wool, leave the wool on and have it tanned.

◆ If it is long wool, leave the wool on and have it tanned.

The long-wool pelts make marvelous couch throws, or can be made up into pillows. (In pillows, the most economical use is to have the pelt on one side only, using fabric for the other side.)

Saddle Pads from Pelts

Tanned pelts can be used to make saddle pads to protect a horse's back from the saddle. Wool absorbs moisture and allows some circulation of air under the saddle. To make a saddle pad, place the pelt on the horse, wool side down. Put the saddle on top of it. With a felt-tip liner, outline the saddle about ½ inch out from the saddle edge. Make another outline 1½ inches further out, so you can turn up the edges for a fleecy outline around the edge. This outline can be trimmed off where necessary to allow the girth to lay flat.

Sulfuric-Acid Tanning:
An Australian Home-Tanning Recipe

If you want to do your own tanning, here's a method from Australia that works well for a home or farm setting.

Working outdoors, use a large, enamel, stainless steel, or other tub that will not be damaged or react with sulfuric acid. An old porcelain bathtub would do.

Put into the tub 8 cups of pickling salt, pour 2 gallons of boiling water over the salt, and stir to dissolve. In a large bucket, pour 1½ gallons of boiling water over 8 cups of raw bran flakes. Let this soak for an hour, then strain it into the salt water. Add 1 ounce of sulfuric acid for each gallon of liquid, working very carefully with the acid.

Put the pelt, which has been cleaned of flesh and gently

washed, into the mixture. When it is saturated, stir it occasionally and let it soak for about 30 minutes. Remove it from the solution and gently stretch the pelt out to dry, skin side down, on a drying frame, nailing or stapling it to the frame. Give the skin side a coat of neat's-foot oil. When it is dry, rub the skin side with a wire brush till it is softened. Then comb up the wool and brush it gently with a hair brush. The softness and sheen of the wool can be improved by using VO-5 hairdressing; rub a small amount on your hands and run your hands through the brushed wool.

You'll find tanneries and tanning suppliers listed in "Sources."

Quilt Batts and Mattress Covers

Quilting has enjoyed a real renaissance in the last few years, so much so that specialty shops are springing up to sell only pure cotton fabrics for that use. *The Wall Street Journal* had a front-page article about the great popularity of quilts and the fantastic prices that were being charged, especially by decorators, for special-ordered handmade quilts. Whether they are considered decorator items or simply comforters, quilts are the "in" thing. While there is a certain practicality in stuffing them with polyester-fiberfill batts, which are more washable, these chemical fillings cannot compete with wool for exceptional warmth and insulating quality, not to mention wool's greater resistance to fire. Wool is, of course, warmer in winter, but a wool-filled quilt is still usable — and cool — in the summer, due to that same insulating feature.

There is a certain incongruity in making a beautiful handmade quilt of pure cotton, then filling it with polyester. For a washable quilt with a wool batt, the batt needs only to be quilted inside plain muslin sheets, then the pieced quilt slid over it like a huge pillowslip that can be taken off and washed.

A new quilt-related item that is gaining in popularity is a mattress cover of plain wool batting inside a muslin cover. It is used over the mattress, under the sheet, for warmth and comfort. The ones that I saw advertised had a price tag of over $200.

Owners of Patrick Green's Cottage Industry carder are finding that quilters can constitute quite a sizable portion of their market, once they let it be known that they do the carding of wool quilt batts. The customers can be reached by advertising, or by joining a quilters' group, learning the craft, and offering batts either encased in muslin (in sizes made to order) or just plain batts. Teaching quilting and/or lecturing on quilts is another way to reach customers. Contact shops that sell cotton quilt fabrics to let them know that the pure wool batting is available.

Local regulations may prevent store sales of batts without a license ("concealed stuffing" laws differ from state to state), but a batt that is not encased in muslin should be legal to sell. Most states require that the seller have a concealed-stuffing license, purchased annually, in order to make and sell quilts, pillows, upholstery, or any stuffed items (wool or otherwise).

As to selling wool-filled quilts, you might check your local regulations on farm businesses. Usually local laws allow the sale of "farm products" directly from the farm without a license, and this might include wool-filled quilts.

Consider the many items that can be made from quilted material, such as pillow covers, tea cozies, Christmas stockings, potholders, and placemats, just for starters. All would be considered superior if wool-stuffed.

Futons

Futons are becoming a potential market for wool. A futon is a traditional type of Japanese bedding, a large thing that is a sort of cross between a mattress and a pillow and a comforter, but intended to be used as a mattress on the floor. Futons can be folded or rolled and put out of the way when not needed for sleeping. The standard sizes vary, but single size is usually 38 inches wide and 80 to 85 inches long. Full size is 55 inches wide. For queen and king size, 60 to 80 inches wide would be luxurious and most fashionable.

For use as bed coverings, futons can be made the same thickness as quilts; for mattresses they should be thicker, or two of them can be used together.

The traditional stuffing has been cotton, but the most popular ones now use wool. To make a wool-stuffed futon, spread the wool batting onto an inside-out muslin "pillow slip" the size of the desired futon, then tack the batting at the corners and down the center. Turn the muslin cover right side out, with the batting inside it, sew up the open end, and carefully quilt or tuft the entire futon. An outer cover of a washable Japanese print makes a wonderful cover around the futon, and it can be either zippered for easy removal or sewn at one end and the stitches removed when the cover needs washing.

If the futon is to serve alternate use as soft furniture when rolled or folded in thirds, a cover of upholstery or drapery fabric would be suitable.

Making Wool Felt and Felt Objects

The unique structure of wool fibers, with their outer scaly surface, is what makes felting possible. A combination of heat, moisture, friction, and pressure can cause the scales to interlock. Depending on the depth of the layers of wool being used, a thin or a thick felt can be obtained.

Industry makes great quantities of felt of various kinds for such uses as hats, slippers, and carpet pads, plus many and varied manufacturing uses. These are all made from waste wool that is not usable for other purposes.

Feltmaking has developed into a very popular art form among wool craftspeople in recent years. It is being used for handcrafted functional items as well as three-dimensional sculptures, unusual wall hangings, and small novelties.

This is all of special interest to wool sellers, as some of the lower grades of wool are particularly suitable for felting. Wools that have been overly weathered will felt better than those not excessively weathered. Some of the fine wools, with a high number of barbs or serrations per fiber, felt better than the long-luster wools.

Karakul and part-Karakul fleeces, because of their combination of long and short fibers within the fleece, are sometimes almost felted into fleece rugs even before they are sheared, especially under extreme climatic conditions or high rainfall. I know of one Karakul raiser who keeps aside the fleeces that show the most felting, and felts them even more, for sale as rugs.

Felting can be done as a first step in making a product or be the end product. There are quite a few felting techniques, but most felters develop their own methods to fit in with their work space and facilities, then invent the product to suit the technique that is most convenient for their own situations.

The most common felting techniques make use of

◆ A washing machine and dryer
◆ Hot water, cold water, and rubbing
◆ Rolling, kneading, and rubbing
◆ Soap, hot water, and rubbing

Several good books and booklets on felting (see "Sources") describe the processes and illustrate what is being done in that field. The variety of things that can be made with handmade

Working with felt, you can make a variety of appealing, wool-based products. These, done on a Louet felting board, are only the beginning.

felt is quite unbelievable, and limited only by your imagination.

If felting really interests you, the possibilities seem greater than for almost any other wool process. A good, flat felt can be used in place of fabric (but for felted garments, the flat felt must be expertly made). Many shaped felt objects can be made without sewing. For example:

Small Items	*Large Items*
Slippers	Saddle blankets
Shaped or cut-and-sewn mittens	Table pads
	Felt-and-quilted placemats
Boots with rubber soles (use a special process with retread rubber)	Cushion covers
	Wall hangings
	Wine carboy jackets
Insoles	Rugs (elegant with fringe and crocheted edges)
Hot pads	
Cork pads or tiles with felt bottoms	Blankets made of squares sewn, embroidered, or crocheted together
Beads for jewelry	Garments: jackets, vests, coats
Balls for Christmas ornaments	Garments made from felt that is shaped during felting, then tailored
Large balls for cat toys	Museum-quality doll bodies made completely from felt, and clothed in felt
Tea cozies	
Hats	
Eyeglass cases	Crib pads
Felt-and-leather handbags	Chair pads for invalids

Selling Wool for Feltmaking

So, how do you get started selling wool to felters? You can advertise, which is the obvious way, but costs money and may not locate enough people who are interested. Or, you can get into feltmaking yourself. You will then meet other felters who will become wool customers. Investigate the different processes for making felt, read books, attend classes. Try to develop a specialty that will make you sufficiently well known so that you can give lessons (to make new customers for wool) and give talks about feltmaking. Work up some felted object that you can offer for sale; this is wool-related income and, in addition, often a means of bringing in customers for wool and for lessons so that they can copy your product. Christmas ornament classes would be ideal, as this is a seasonal project, and many people will be interested at that particular time.

Wool will felt readily in the grease, so you have a choice of whether to wash or not wash the wool before using it for felting. Since soap and water are used during the feltmaking, it is faster, for many items, if you omit the washing prior to felting, knowing that the wool will be washed by the time it is felted anyway. Home soap-makers will want to try a mutton-tallow soap, made as a soft soap, for their felting process. A combination of a powered picker and a feltmaking machine (see "Sources" for both) could make use of washed or unwashed wool for a cottage industry in feltmaking.

Other Uses of Wool

Many imaginative small items can be made from wool, wool yarn, carded wool, and felt. One small enterprise makes wool plant dusters. The owners buy the raw wool, wash and card it on the Cottage Industry carder, and make plant dusters as well as Christmas ornaments and wool novelties. Other small wool items could include

◆ Dusting mittens (yarn pompoms sewn to the palms of soft cotton gloves or mittens)
◆ Sheep-shaped hand puppets made of felt, yarn, wool, or shearling pelt
◆ Lamp shades: a wire frame wound with wool yarn
◆ Balls of felt to be hung as crib toys, with sculptured faces or other decoration
◆ Novelty greeting cards decorated with wool and sheep drawings
◆ Woolly sheep-shaped refrigerator magnets
◆ Baskets combining handspun yarn with traditional basket materials
◆ Dog or cat pillows: woolen (or burlap) bags filled with washed skirtings

Business and Merchandising Tips

Finances

THE ESSENCE OF A COTTAGE INDUSTRY is work translated into income. The best advice is not to borrow to start. However, if you feel you *have* to borrow, you will need to make a good presentation to support your request. This will include information you have determined by research, i.e., projected income versus expenses.

Ideally, your basic capital is the hours you are willing to invest. To offset time, try to accumulate equipment that saves time or makes money. Purchase the level of equipment you can initially afford.

In business, as in life, there are the cautious and there are the gamblers. The cautious ones work long, hard hours, with hand tools, to accumulate the savings to purchase larger equipment. It takes a while, but it is the safe way. This approach insures that the business can support itself. The beauty of creating a business this way is that you learn thoroughly and become recognized as an authority. Income-producing tools and salable inventory are the two best investments you can make.

Purchasing equipment is always a risk, but less so if it

comes from business savings. Many of the businesses that started during the early '80s failed because they gambled on the good times and borrowed funds to buy equipment or, even worse, for operating expenses.

When in debt, the slightest financial hitch, such as a momentary lull in sales, can throw you into a depressed mood that makes daily production difficult. This is a small disaster in itself, for you depend on being a self-starter when you are self-employed. Avoid the things that you know can paralyze your motivation. The essence of cottage industry is independence, and debt undermines that independence. A cottage industry is also a labor of love. You don't want a stranger in on your love affair, so be cautious of money lenders — also of partners, who can become quite vocal if their funds appear to be endangered.

Judy Lewman in her office at Spring Creek Farm. The business end of a cottage industry is as important as the product.

Facilities

It is wise, for a number of reasons, to establish your business at home, to achieve a true cottage-industry environment. Rented quarters often present severe problems regarding hours of work, cost of modification, available space, access at all times, and, above all, high rent that takes the cream off the top. Also, there is a greater risk of theft and vandalism when you do not live on the premises. The time taken in commuting to a shop away from home is time taken out of your life, which is time that can never be replaced. All of us must value this time above all else. When you are working at home, you can do more than one thing at once; you can have dinner cooking while you are working, you can be baking bread while you card wool, you can chop wood while wool is soaking in the hot water and detergent for wool washing. There are many things that take time but do not need your constant personal attention. When two people are occupied in earning a living at home, even more options are possible because of their cooperation. It will be worth your while to learn to make adjustments in your scheduling in order to get more accomplished with less time and effort, on your own property.

Protecting Your Investment

One thing that must be considered is the value of your equipment and processing facility. These should be insured, for their loss would put you completely out of business, particularly if you could not afford to replace them. In some cases, insurance for your equipment can be added to a general homeowners' policy.

For another kind of protection, put lock-out as well as disconnect attachments on your power equipment; these will prevent children from doing any damage — either to themselves or the machinery.

Documentation

Complete financial documentation is essential for any business enterprise. If you keep sheep, you also need detailed livestock records, which are described on page 42.

Financial records consist of sales on one side, balanced by expenses on the other side. What is left over is your profit. Use of a "creative" accountant is recommended. Keep track of every expense, even fringe expenses, and let the accountant put them in perspective. Maintain records, month by month, of expenses for stationery, stamps, phone calls, car or truck mileage, equipment and maintenance, everything. If you're raising sheep, keep track, separately, of farm expenses such as sheep purchases, fence supplies, veterinary supplies, grain and hay — all the things connected with raising sheep, shearing sheep, and selling them.

These records are necessary for income-tax purposes for a cottage industry, but, in addition, they will show you if you are actually making a profit. *The Black Sheep Newsletter* had a series of three articles covering the U.S. federal income taxation for sheep owners. The last article, in the spring 1984 issue (number 38/39), discussed proving a profit motive, which is extremely important. If the government decides to call your business a hobby, then the burden of proof is on you — you must prove that it is in fact a business with the intent of making a profit. Nothing is deductible if you cannot prove that your business *is* a business.

Incentive Payments for Wool Growers

In the United States, incentive payments, which are made in accordance with the National Wool Act, are price-support payments, not funded directly from tax revenues but from a tariff charged on all lamb and mutton imported into the United States.

The size of the payment is that required to raise the national *average* price received by all U.S. producers of shorn wool, up to the announced incentive price. Your County Agricultural Cooperative Extension Service usually has the forms that sheepraisers must fill out annually and return prior to January 31 regarding wool sold the previous year. In February of every year the percentage is computed, and payments made about April. The percentage fluctuates from year to year.

The 1982 incentive support price level announced in February 1983 was $1.53 per pound, meaning if the national *average* price was less than $1.53 a pound in 1982, an incentive payment would be made. Since the 1982 average wool price was 61.3 cents per pound, the wool incentive rate was set at 149.6 percent of the net proceeds of their raw wool sales for all those who filed.

As an example of how it worked that year: If you had 100 pounds of wool and sold them for 50 cents per pound, you would be paid 149.6 percent of the $50 you received for your wool — $74.80. But if you sold your 100 pounds of wool for $2.00 a pound, by keeping the fleece clean and carefully sheared, and located handspinners who were happy to pay more than 50 cents a pound for your good wool, you would have received $200 for the wool sold and then an incentive payment of $299.20. This shows that there is one more good reason to sell your wool for the best price.

When you sell each fleece, you must get the signature of the buyer and the date, on a sales slip, to prove the wool sale and the price paid. If you use your own wool rather than selling it, there is of course no incentive payment.

Pricing

Prices must be high enough to give you a good return and low enough to be competitive. Review your prices periodically to be sure you are not offering one item at a loss. If, overall, you are making a profit, you may not realize that certain items are not contributing to this profit.

Be realistic about prices; consider *all* related expenses when pricing. You cannot *completely* determine a price from adding up expenses, so you may need to limit expenses to keep the price in line with what you know you can charge.

Be aware of all considerations. In selling washed wool, for instance, you must pay careful attention to the loss of weight that takes place during washing to make sure you price the processed wool accordingly, in proper relation to what you charge for unwashed wool.

Your Own Logo

Regular and effective promotion is essential. Start by establishing a logo to appear in all of your ads, catalogs, stationery, and labels. A simple original drawing will suffice, but be sure you do not copy another person's logo. You may want to change your basic ad from time to time to be sure it is noticed and read. But the logo should remain the same.

Advertising

The size, extent, and cost of your advertising should be in proportion to your capability to handle the responses to the ad. One large ad in a leading publication could spell trouble, as would advertising placed in too many publications. A deluge of responses may be very satisfying, but it can put you in the position of being slow in replying to inquiries. Correspondence and paperwork in general use up the time in which you could be filling orders. In responding to mail, you should

Easily recognizable logos.

◆ Answer the day you get the letter (letters can pile up quickly)
◆ Have letterhead paper (it need not be expensive, just look businesslike)
◆ Type, or write very legibly (this is also part of the business impression you give)
◆ Be polite and friendly (even if rushed, don't sound abrupt)
◆ Be exact (this can save an additional letter and stamp, as well as time)

An unusual ploy in advertising would be actually to promote your second-quality wool for specific purposes such as felting and textured yarn. Appeal to cost savings, and point out that the wool is superior for the particular use for which it is being recommended.

Try to plan your advertising to encourage those with a

serious interest in your product rather than people writing out of curiosity. Select the publications you advertise in on this basis also. Many businesses, when indicating their return addresses, use different box numbers or department numbers in different publications, to see which ads are most productive.

When advertising "sample cards available, $2" (or whatever price) have cards ready before the ad appears. With continual requests you will run out of cards sooner or later, but at least start out by being ahead. When you run out, let requests pile up and make cards to fill them periodically. A month would be a reasonable wait — much longer and you get complaints.

Co-op ads, in conjunction with another wool seller, could help ease the cost and share the burden of paperwork, as well as dividing up the orders to be filled. Advertising as a joint venture can make it possible to place a larger ad than would be warranted for the business of only one person, and the larger space has a greater impact on the potential customers. Selling raw wool? Advertise with another wool seller in your area. If you raise different wool types, then orders would go to the person able to fill them. Selling handspun yarn? Get together with several spinners to advertise. Divide the sample requests and divide the orders. This can be a great help if each spinner has chosen one type of order to fill; this could be according to yarn size, white or dark wool, texture, one-ply or two-ply yarns. This kind of cooperation gives many of the benefits of a partnership with few of the problems. There is nothing final or binding about this advertising relationship, it is just voluntary cooperation. If the cost is moderate, one order could pay for your share of it. In the event of too many orders, you are working together with someone who could take excess orders and fill them.

Selling to Shops

The *Craft Report* (see "Sources") is one of the few periodicals that is primarily concerned with the *business* of crafts, and directed to both shops and craftspeople. Their "Crafts Wanted" section is a good place to scout out shops and galleries that are definitely in the market for merchandise, and it specifies just what type of articles they are seeking. They print pages and pages of "Shows and Fairs," listed by the state in which they will be held. Their "Marketplace" classified ads are listed by topics, such as "Fiber Supplies" and "Fabric Supplies." There is also a "Crafts Available" section in which to advertise, also by topic, such as "Quilts," "Fiber," and "Clothing." These ads are not expensive and reach a wide range of markets. The *Crafts Report* would be a good place to take out a small ad for handspun yarn or woven garments. Be prepared to quote two different prices, one for consignment, and one for outright sale. Consignment will probably be suggested only in regard to yarn purchase, not wool. On consignment sales, you normally get about 60 percent of the retail price. (For consignment contracts and related information, see *Handspinner's Guide to Selling* in "Sources.") On cash sales, shops usually pay 50 percent of the retail price they will be asking. If your wholesale price is so high that they could not double it, they would not likely be interested in buying. Type out your prices and information and have them reproduced by offset or even photocopy; either one looks more businesslike than a handwritten price list.

Instead of magazine advertising, you can contact shops directly. Look in the leading fiber magazines and write to the shops that are advertising in these magazines. It is not good policy to send wool samples or sample cards of yarn unrequested. In your letter, offer samples. If a shop requests a sample card and additional information, the shop manager will be looking for it when it arrives, and give more attention than if it came unrequested.

Once you start supplying a shop, it is important to be reliable and fill orders promptly, even ahead of your retail orders. The shop needs merchandise to sell in order to stay in business. If the shop's staff promotes your product and then is unable to get it from you, they have put themselves in a very bad position. Be a reliable supplier.

Advertising to Weavers and Spinners

Both *SpinOff* and *Handwoven* magazines (see "Sources") publish a page or more of weavers' and spinners' guilds and news of their events and projects. While this information is not intended as a mailing list to be used to sell products, it does tell which guilds have newsletters, and you could write to those guilds and take out small ads in their little publications. The cost of those ads would be extremely low.

The Handweavers Guild of America (see "Sources") publishes an HGA Educational Directory. It lists a great number of schools, shops, and private teachers giving lessons or classes or workshops in weaving, spinning, and related fiberwork. This is available from the Handweavers Guild of America, which also publishes the magazine *Shuttle, Spindle and Dyepot.* This directory would give you a good mailing list for selling carded wool or handspun yarn.

Producing a Catalog

Even if you're offering only a handful of products, you'll probably want to have them described in print. Customers need to have something to refer to — your catalog or price list.

Start with a modest catalog, reproduced in small quantity by offset or photocopy. From the interest shown by responses, you will probably see changes that you should make in the future. Make the catalog clear and legible, personal and attractive, but not necessarily expensive. Rule out slick paper and full color; the expense is not warranted. If possible, use drawings rather than photographs. Drawings reproduce well and at less expense than photographs, but the choice will depend on your access to attractive drawings.

Have your prices on a separate page so that only one page will need to be updated. This also allows you the option of putting in different price lists, depending on whether you are sending the catalog to a retail or a wholesale customer.

Selling Directly to Customers

Do your homework to discover where you can most likely find customers for your wool or whatever wool product you are selling.

Contact spinning guilds and ask if you can present a program about sheep and wool, and show them samples of your fleece. This will require a well-planned presentation, a high level of knowledge of the subject matter, and fleece that is sufficiently clean to be impressive.

At any sheep shows that are on your agenda, make a special effort to appeal to spinners. Show your cleanest wool in baskets with price tags that say "Choice Handspinning Wool." Have smaller signs offering felting wool, locker lambs, breeding stock, whatever you sell. Approach spinners at county fairs. Offer to supply fleeces for their Sheep-to-Shawl contests, as long as you are sure your fleeces are really good. If you don't supply contest fleeces, at least show the spinners generous samples, so they can see the quality and have a chance to make the comparison between yours and what they are using.

To sell handspun yarn and articles made from wool or yarn, enter craft fairs. A shared booth at a craft fair or craft conference works well if those who share the booth have different but compatible, complementary merchandise, such as wool and yarn, yarn and garments. In addition to sharing costs, this allows more flexibility and freedom — you can get away from the booth from time to time for lunch, the restroom, and errands.

Tailgate sales and flea markets are other places to sell, if you have enough variety of merchandise to make it worth while. Be sure you comply with local license and tax laws.

Craft Shows and Street Fairs

Shows and fairs are good places to get your work seen initially by the public. In general, low-priced articles will sell best. Appearing at a public selling event will give you the chance to hand out price lists and brochures, and to see how people respond to your products. The first time you try to sell may not be successful, but if you observe reactions and listen to comments and see how other craftspeople handle their sales, it could be a valuable experience.

Be sure to read the section on selling at fairs on page 106. In addition, keep in mind these general tips for making your craft fair displays successful:

◆ Have brochures or catalogs to hand out — not expensive ones, but attractive.

◆ Take a variety of merchandise, all priced and labelled. Have care instructions on labels for wool garments.

◆ Be prepared for inclement weather with tarps, plastic, nails, and a hammer.

◆ Be dressed comfortably and suitably for a variety of kinds of weather.

◆ Have an assistant, at least most of the time, or you can't even go to the restroom.

◆ Bring a cash box and change — also pens. Keep the cash box safely out of reach. Remove large bills to a safer place as needed.

◆ Have healthy snacks and a jug of cold water.

◆ Inquire ahead to see if you need to bring sales books or if these are provided.

◆ Have plenty of merchandise, since customers like to have a good selection from which to choose. An abundant display creates more interest.

◆ Have items in a wide price range — something for every pocketbook.

◆ Check the sales record of the fair as well as the number of years it's been in existence. Well-juried fairs sell best. Long-established shows run smoother. Good advertising is necessary in order to guarantee good attendance.

◆ If there is a high booth fee and no commission, decide how much merchandise you could reasonably hope to sell, and figure out if this would warrant the fee required. If there is no booth fee, only a commission, then no sales would require no payment. You might be disappointed with low sales, but at least the commission taken would also be small.

The Home Studio Shop

A rustic roadside stand, in a rural area that is frequented by tourists, might be a good marketplace. This would be similar to a small studio, open at the ringing of a bell rather than regular hours.

Many a shop has started with home sales, developed into an informal home/studio salesroom, and finally graduated to a separate, full-grown shop. When the shop can be on your own property, it makes a more flexible situation with easier hours and no commuting. Having the same phone number for the shop and your residence may bother you with calls at all hours, but you do not miss the important calls. In the beginning, particularly, each call is a potential customer.

Whether your business is a shop or a scouring-picking-carding service such as Amazing Acres, be sure that anyone driving by knows that you're there.

A small shop can and should carry other things in addition to your own merchandise. You might supply the wool for sale, and yarn or fabric or garments made from it, but you need even more variety than this, if the shop is to pay its way. If your own supply

At Wool and Feathers, Gisela Gminder's main product is yarn from local sheep, but she is not dependent on that alone. Her shop offers a wide variety of handspun and handcrafted items, as well as supplies for those who want to do the spinning and handwork themselves. Posted in the midst of a tempting selection of yarns is a sign advertising yet another product: locker lamb in whatever cuts a customer might request.

ASK
GISELA OR SUSAN
ABOUT CUSTOM RAISED
LAMB
READY FOR YOUR FREEZER
FROM AUGUST ON

of wool is limited, you could carry wool on consignment from other growers.

It is nice if most of the things are sheep- or wool-oriented. These could be books; sheep-imprinted stationery, napkins, or fabric; or spinning and weaving supplies, dyes, and some small items. Start with a small inventory and expand as demand requires. Be careful about investing in looms unless you are an experienced weaver and unless you can afford to tie up a lot of money in a product that is expensive and moves slowly. Looms are in a competitive field that is often dominated by the larger mail-order businesses.

Any family talent should be exploited. Do you have a family member who is good at drawing, silk screening, or photography? Reproduce that person's work as postcards or notepaper to sell in your studio/shop.

Don't neglect the "Locker Lamb Available" sign in your shop. Gisela Gminder of Wool and Feathers in Vermont gets a good response to this sign that is now permanently displayed in her store, which sells yarn, wheels, garments, pelts, books, toys, buttons, and all kinds of wool-related merchandise.

In selling handspun yarn, have a good quantity on display. A big pile of yarn attracts attention. If the customers cannot see the colors of the yarn underneath, they must handle the yarn, and the feel of handspun is irresistible. The irresistibility of products is important. Handspun yarn? It must be attractive and labelled and displayed well. The customer does not necessarily want it just because you say it is handspun, or may not even know the difference between handspun and factory-made "homespun" (which is simply a legal term for 1-ply mill yarn that is an imitation of handspun). Handwoven? To be irresistible, never forget the competition, it must be more attractive than the factory product.

Lessons

Lessons? Be sure that your shop offers classes. Spinning lessons create wool customers. If necessary, hire teachers; you need instructors who are qualified and experienced. Knitting classes create yarn customers. Felting classes create wool customers. Have a quilting class where beginners make small quilted articles and use wool or handmade felt to stuff them: tea cozies, placemats, quilted pillow tops, and whatever other small items capture the imagination. To beginners, a small project sounds less intimidating and leads to larger projects.

Public Relations

What attracts customers? Initially, customers are attracted by three main factors: price, quality, and ease of purchase. Prices may not be as important as you would think. Many people will cheerfully pay more to get exactly what they want, to get a superior product, and to deal with the person they enjoy.

Attracting repeat customers takes personality, reliability of supply (continuity), integrity, and good value. Know your product well, and talk about it. People want to feel that the vendor is qualified and can offer advice as well as good service. When selling a service, if you promise something for a certain date, you should either deliver on time and at the agreed price, or advise the customer ahead of time regarding the problem. Repeat customers are the best advertising.

Why do *you* go back to a particular store or vendor? Your answer to this question should have an impact on the way you conduct your own business.

Equipment

CHOOSING THE RIGHT EQUIPMENT for a new enterprise is difficult, since one is never quite sure whether an item is suitable until it has been in use for a while.

However modest or ambitious your cottage industry, you can make no better investment than quality tools. This chapter is intended to detail what I consider to be the most useful equipment now available — tools that are well made, reliable, and efficient, and that can be depended on during long hard use. This section is not intended as a complete catalog, and could possibly be considered biased, but I have listed the equipment I have worked with and can recommend. I have been very selective, because it is so important to get the best.

Although it is tempting to quote prices in the interests of offering complete information, I have not because of the price changes that inflation and exchange rates can cause, even in a short time. Suppliers of all the equipment described here are listed in "Sources," and a short note to a supplier with a stamped, self-addressed envelope will result in up-to-date prices as well as any new information about a particular piece of equipment.

Carders

Table-top Drum Carder

The majority of handspinners, up to thirty years ago, were using hand cards to prepare their wool for spinning. This was quite time-consuming and hard on their hands. The availability of reasonably priced, table-top drum carders helped to popularize handspinning.

The table-top carder is adequate for the individual spinner, and a good starting tool for a small business, allowing the business to develop to the point where larger equipment is warranted. Kay Fielding started her Custom Colors business by layering and blending dyed, exotic fibers on a drum carder, gradually expanding her sales to an international market before purchasing a Jumbo Exotic carder.

A drum carder has only two carding rollers, is hand turned, and clamps to the table top. Its size means it can easily be stored away. Patrick Green makes three models of standard drum carders, a heavy-duty Deluxe carder of heirloom quality (shown on page 51) with interchangeable drums for processing all wools and exotics, a Beverly Deluxe with a two-speed feature for difficult fibers and blends, and a Homestyle "barewood" economy version for common wools. All models have British carding cloth such as that supplied to the woolen-mill trade, with a 5-ply, ⅛-inch thick, vulcanized rubber-fabric backing. Production rate with a drum carder would be about a pound of wool an hour.

Carder for Exotic Fibers

For those fiber artists who specialize in fine wools and exotic fibers, such as super-fine Merino, Angora bunny, kid mohair, silk, cashmere, llama, and musk-ox, Patrick Green has introduced several new carding cloths for the interchangeable carder drums — a "Fur" drum to do bunny, bunny blends, and most other exotics; a "320" drum for advanced blending; a new high-profile Merino drum for Merino and Rambouillet; and an outstanding Super-Merino drum for superfine Merino and

Sharlea wools, which are ordinarily so difficult to card without noils. These interchangeable drums all have their place on the carding bench of the perfectionist. Both the Deluxe and the Beverly Deluxe carders have the special infeed roll necessary for the proper carding action with the specialized drums.

Table-top Rover for Continuous Roving

This seven-drum, powered, table-top carding machine was designed for the author's studio, and is the perfect carder for a production spinner or for a sheepraiser who wishes to market the choicest wools. Good-quality, picked wool makes a lovely, well-formed roving, automatically wound into a center-pull "bump" (ball) for spinning. Two or more dyed wools can be fed side by side for a delightful ribbon of colors. Production rate is about 4 or 5 pounds per hour, depending on the fiber. Minimum fiber length for this carder is about 3 inches — it just loves the longer wools, up to 6 inches. Machine size is 4 feet long, 2 feet wide, and 1½ feet high; it weighs about 200 pounds. Made to order with ½-HP motor, wired for 110 volts, with a switch at each end of the machine. This is the smallest of the continuous carders made by Patrick Green.

The Cottage Industry Carders

The Cottage Industry carders were developed by Patrick Green specifically for the small entrepreneur. They are sturdy, well-built machines that can handle the long-staple wools used by handspinners, medium-length and moderately short wools, as well as adult mohair. Some models are customized for exotic blends in addition to wool.

These carders are all built from industrial-quality materials, all powered shafts are ball-bearing mounted with V-belt drives, and powered with ½-HP or ¾-HP motors. The carding drums are 16 inches wide and are clothed with commercial carding cloth.

The Economy basic model has seven carding drums, a flycomb, and a large storage roll, and can produce a batt 6

Paula's Rover, a continuous seven-drum roving carder for the artisan (shown without its safety side guards).

feet long that can be removed while the machine is in operation. In addition, it can be quickly converted to continuous roving (sliver) production and has a take-away belt to elevate the fluffy roving and let it coil into a large container.

The Jumbo model, which can be customized for wool and/ or exotics, has nine carding drums including a main cylinder twice the size of the Economy model, flycomb, large storage roll, and a bumpwinder section that automatically winds the compact roving into a center-pull ball for easy storage or shipment, and convenience in spinning. Production rate for wool: 8 to 12 pounds per hour.

Wool must be well washed before carding and have been teased through a wool picker. These carders are the ideal equipment for owners of small flocks who want to process wool for sale to spinners, and also do custom carding in their own area or by mail. All models are about 45 inches high, 30 inches wide, and vary from 60 to 75 inches long, depending on customizing. Weight would be from about 450 pounds to 900 pounds, uncrated.

Wool Pickers

A good picker (which teases wool prior to carding) is a necessity for anyone who is selling clean, carded wool. If wool is not picked before you use the small drum carder, you can damage the carding cloth; if wool is not picked before you use the Cottage Industry carder, the machine does not do as good a carding job, and you risk doing some damage to the wool as well as to the carder. Unteased (unpicked) wool does not card well and the staple length may be shortened.

Paula's Picker

This cradle-type wool picker is a continuous-process machine, that passes the wool from the front to the rear, where it can drop into a box or container. Fed properly (restraining the

The Jumbo Cottage Industry carder with a bump winder (shown with safety guards removed). Can make either 6-foot batts or compact roving, which is automatically wound into a "bump" for easy shipping and carefree spinning.

wool rather than pushing it into the teeth), it will tease and/or blend wool prior to carding. Production rate would be about a pound in five minutes. Most of the dirt and small seeds will fall through the slits between the bottom pads and can be brushed off the table when you are done. The bottom teeth pads can be vacuumed or brushed periodically to keep the resulting teased wool cleaner.

When you are using the picker, wool is placed on the front slope in such a way that it is picked up gradually as you swing the top cradle. As you feed it, the wool should be restrained by one hand to get a good picking action and to be sure the picker does not grab too much wool at a time. The picker teeth are placed in a particular pattern that causes the wool to work progressively through the machine so it comes out of the other end all teased.

Safety: The ground, polished, and hardened picker points are smooth and sharp like needles, to do a beautiful job of picking. These points must be treated with respect, the ma-

Paula's Picker. Wool should be teased in a picker before carding, and this hand-operated picker does an excellent job with small batches of wool. Note use of leather bib.

chine operated in accordance with directions, and locked when not in use. There is a place to put a padlock to protect children or unauthorized people from playing with it. For safety, we recommend that you wear a leather bib apron and a close-fitting leather glove on the hand that feeds the fibers. Paula's Picker, with 194 picking points, is sold in "bare-wood" mahogany, for economy. The cradle of both models swings in fall bearings.

Special Triple Picker

This elegant Hardrock Maple picker, nicely finished, has over three times as many picker points as the standard Paula's Picker, ultra-smooth and polished points in a density that is perfect for exotic and fine fibers, as well as for long wools and mohair. It is especially impressive on kid mohair, picking it into a fluffy cloud suitable for spinning direct from the picker. It is also excellent for blending dyed colors and exotic fibers with wool. This model is ideal for a beginning cottage industry to use until the pressure of volume requires the Powered Picker.

Patrick's Powered Picker

Patrick Green is offering a machine-powered wool picker designed specifically to handle the types of wool desired by handspinners. Its gentle action coupled with controlled air currents "opens" the wool to a fluffy state and blows it into a picked-wool enclosure behind the machine. It has a moving infeed belt and is economically powered by a ¾-HP motor. Production is around 30 pounds an hour.

The powered picker is particularly useful to owners of the Cottage Industry carder, who require a picker with greater capacity than Paula's Picker, which is hand powered. This picker does a beautiful job of blending natural colors or dyed colors to obtain a larger quantity of a shade than would otherwise be available and, with equal success, it can blend exotic fibers with wool. Many combinations can be spun directly from the picker, without further processing.

Above, Patrick's Powered Picker can prepare about 30 pounds of wool per hour. At the left, the Louet carder board, hand-operated with a forward rolling motion, is especially good for wools with very long fibers or for blending dyed fibers.

The picker is 48 inches long, 24 inches wide, 48 inches high; shipping weight is 550 pounds. Available from Patrick Green.

Louet Carder Board

The Louet carder board is really a combination of a picker and hand cards, not either one but giving somewhat the same effect as both (but slower). You use it like a rolling pin, rolling it away from you, but *not* back and forth.

To use it, load the bottom

carding board with wool that you want to card/pick, and pass the roller across it, ending with an upward motion. Lift up the roller and roll again, repeating until the wool is nicely prepared. You can process either clean or greasy wool. This tool is especially good for wools with very long fibers that cannot be processed easily with other equipment. It is also good for blending dyed fibers and can be quickly cleaned between colors.

Drying Equipment

Centrifugal Extractors

Most wool is washed, sooner or later, and after it is washed, the water must be removed. One of the most efficient ways to do this is with a high-speed centrifugal extractor. There is more than one manufacturer of centrifugal extractors for commercial use, the best known being Bock. The machines are made in several sizes (capacities), and one of the two smallest ones should suffice for cottage-industry use. Extractors are all sturdily made and require little maintenance. Hand-spinners can use extractors to remove wash water and rinse water, leaving the yarn with just enough moisture for the blocking process. For anyone washing raw wool, an extractor is not only useful, it is necessary.

A centrifugal extractor is faster and better for spinning out excess water from washed wool than the spin cycle of most home washing machines.

There are often real bargains to be found in used extractors. Inquire of laundry-equipment companies (see the Yellow Pages for the nearest large city) or look in second-hand stores that handle appliances and equipment.

A second, but less efficient, option would be to use a

spinner-type washing machine. It could be used to soak the wool, then to spin out the wash and rinse waters. However, the average household machine does not spin fast enough to remove as much moisture as an extractor. One exception is the small Hoover washer/spinner combination, with a smaller than average capacity but a faster speed. A used Hoover could be kept solely for wool use, and would not even need to be connected to water, just to power, for the spinner portion.

Drying Racks for Wool

Drying racks can be made from almost any mesh or wire that is rustproof. It is convenient to have outdoor racks that can be reassembled indoors for drying wool during wet weather. When space is at a premium, consider stacking the racks with about 8 inches between. See instructions for making the small drying rack table on pages 80-85.

Felting Equipment

The Louet felting board is designed for small items like those in the photograph on page 117. Its size is 20" x 11¾". While an old-fashioned washboard would do essentially the same thing, old washboards are harder to locate. The Louet felting board has an excellent surface for the job. Also available from Louet is an instruction manual for making small items, which has an extremely valuable guide to the shrinkage of items during felting.

Yarn Blockers

A good yarn blocker is a valuable piece of equipment for a handspinner. I have explained the advantage of yarn blocking in my books on spinning, which I assume are familiar to readers. The yarn is wound onto the blocker after washing, to set the twist and dry the yarn under even tension. A blocker is of additional use if it can also be used by weavers as a warping reel.

YARN BLOCKER PLANS

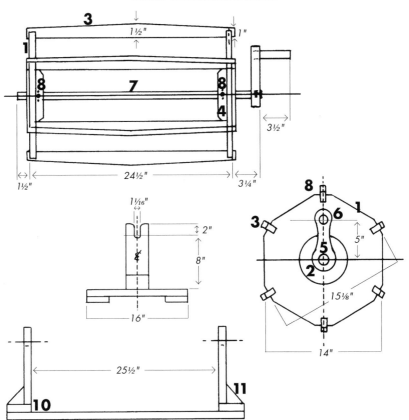

		MATERIALS LIST		
ITEM	NAME	QUANTITY	MATERIAL	LENGTH
1	Reel end	2	¾" plywood, 14" wide	15⅛"
2	Reel spacer	2	¼" plywood, 6" diameter	
3	Reel stretcher	6	1" x 1½", fir or pine	25"
4	Reel hub	2	1¼" x 4", fir or pine	6"
5	Reel crank	1	1¼" x 3, maple	7½"
6	Reel handle	1	¾" dowel, maple	4½"
7	Reel shaft	1	1" steel conduit	29¼"
8	Reel bolts	3	¼" steel, with washers	3½"
9	Reel screws	12	No. 8 steel sheet metal	2"
10	Base frame	assembly	1¼" x 4", fir or pine	
11	Base blocks	2	2½" x 2½", fir or pine	3½"

Note: To use this as a warping reel for a short warp, make the base 3 inches higher, make dowel holes on each end of the reel, and insert 3-inch dowels.

Louet yarn blocker, shown here as a warping reel, with pegs turned outward.

A Make-it-Yourself Blocker

Plans from *Spinning and Weaving with Wool* are given on page 145 for a simple yarn blocker you can make yourself, without the warping reel option, and several makers of blockers are listed in "Sources."

The exact dimensions of a blocker are not important, but the most convenient circumference is about 1½ yards. As to length, you don't want a reel so long that you can't turn the handle while you reach to the further end of the reel; otherwise blocking will require two people. The blocker drum must be made so it can be lifted out of its base so the dry skeins can be slipped off.

Louet Yarn Blocker/Reel

The Louet yarn blocker has a warping-reel option, and can be quickly converted for warping by just turning the pegs outward, as in the photograph. This blocker was unavailable for a time, and spinners will be happy to know that it is again on the market.

Small Looms

Schacht Spindle Company

Schacht makes several small looms that are of interest to beginners and are useful for anyone making small items.

Inkle looms take a warp up to 4½ inches wide and 8½ feet long. The looms are of finely sanded, unfinished hard maple.

Tapestry looms for two-harness tapestry weaving are made of hard maple, finished with Danish oil, and are easily assembled. They are available in 18-inch and 25-inch widths.

Table looms, which are especially good for schools or small projects, come in widths of 15, 20, or 25 inches, with four or eight harnesses. A kit is available for converting table looms to floor looms.

The Pendleton Shop

Another excellent and simple tapestry frame loom is available from the Pendleton Shop.

Louet Sales Company

Louet makes a four-harness, rising-shed table loom with a weaving width of 27½ inches, which can be converted to a floor loom by adding an optional floor stand with four treadles. When not in use, this loom folds to a compact size (34" x 30" x 6¾"), allowing it to be hung on a wall. Its nylon heddles and reed give a very quiet action that makes it ideally suited to workshop and school use.

Floor Looms

There are many floor looms being manufactured in a broad range of prices, and most of them are quite satisfactory. I have detailed here some that I consider to be particularly suitable for use with handspun yarn and that are also reasonably priced.

Schacht Spindle Company

Schacht looms are modestly priced and reliable, with very little assembly necessary when you get them, and with an ease of operation that is difficult to match. Their small floor loom, the Baby Wolf, has a 25-inch weaving width and folds up, even when warped, into such a narrow space (17 inches deep) that it is the ultimate in easily stored looms, while retaining a remarkable structural stability.

Schacht also makes two large, counterbalance looms that I consider excellent, in 36-inch and 45-inch widths. They give a wide shed that is desirable for use with handspun, and are easy to warp, easy to use, and semi-folding. The buyer has a choice of metal or Texsolv heddles.

Schacht four-harness, 45-inch, counterbalance floor loom.

Glimåkra

Glimåkra Looms 'n Yarns has a line of world-renowned countermarche looms in all sizes, and now has a new "Viking" Swedish floor loom, which is a jack loom available in 36- and 48-inch weaving widths, with four harnesses and six treadles. It is solidly constructed, quiet in operation, and gives a clean, even shed. Glimåkra also sells bobbin winders, stainless steel reeds, umbrella swift skeinholders, and shuttles.

Spinning Wheels

There are a great number of spinning wheels on the market — over forty of them are shown in one chapter of my *Spinning and Weaving with Wool*. For a good, efficient wheel at a very affordable price, I usually recommend the Louet, made in Holland and sold throughout Canada, the United States, and Europe.

Louet Spinning Wheel Features

Drive-ratio options. The Louet can be a fast, medium, or slow wheel, whichever you want. You can adjust the wheel speed just by choosing which end of the bobbin you use with the drive belt: you can have a slow drive action by using the larger end of the bobbin, or a medium speed by using the smaller end of the bobbin. In addition to this standard, reversible bobbin (three are provided), there is also a "speed bobbin" available for an even faster drive.

Bobbin-flyer control. One feature that needs to be pointed out is the control you have over the action of the bobbin. For instance, if you should hesitate for a moment at the end of a long draw to pick out a seed or bit of vegetation, you may notice that you have quite enough twist in that length of yarn. You do not need to add any more twist, which is what you would get if you ran the yarn onto the bobbin in the usual manner. With the Louet, all you need to do is touch the flyer arm with one hand, which keeps the flyer from turning. Then, "treadle" the yarn onto the bobbin without letting any more twist enter into it. The yarn, when the flyer arm is detained, zips right onto the bobbin as you treadle.

Inclined orifice. The Louet's large ½-inch orifice allows you to spin bulky yarns but, by being slanted, it also makes it possible to spin fine yarns without the wobble that usually occurs with a large orifice. Also, the orifice size and design makes it easy to thread the wheel

---

Louet statistics:

Orifice: ½ inch, slanted toward
  side exit hole

Single belt, bobbin lead

Simple precision brake adjustment

Bobbin length: 5¼ inches, with nylon
  bearings

Three bobbins, reversible for
  choice of two drive ratios

Flyer width: 4¾ inches, with
  staggered hooks

Drive wheel: 20 inches, drive ratios
  of 5:1 or 7:1 (faster bobbin available for drive ratio of 10:1)

Drive wheel counterbalanced, in
  ball bearings

Built-in lazy Kate

Optional attachable swift (yarn
  winder)

Assembled weight: 20 pounds

Wood: ash and laminated birch;
  nonskid feet. Also available
  in a more classic style in oak.

Effortless heel-and-toe treadle action

Louet spinning wheels. A traditional, rustic oak wheel is at left, and the author is working with a modern S-10 wheel.

quickly without the use of a threading hook.

Synthetic "endless" belt. Even the belt shows the same concern for efficiency. It fits the pulley groove perfectly for maximum traction where needed. Its stretchiness gives the right belt tension on either of the pulley sizes.

Assembly. The Louet is shipped partly disassembled, in a flat box. Even for a person who is doing it for the first time, the spinning wheel is really easy to put together. You just secure two bolts and snap the pitman connection (to the treadle) onto the drive wheel.

Portability. The Louet is sufficiently compact that it will fit into a small car, and is so sturdy that you don't have to worry about it being damaged or out of adjustment when you arrive at your destination. When walking, you can carry it on one arm.

Heel-and-toe treadle. If you previously have used only a Saxony-type treadle, then a very pleasant surprise awaits you when you try Louet's double-action treadle. With it you have control over the action of the drive wheel on both the heel and the toe pressure, allowing you to start the wheel easily. There is not only less effort required, but you are using different sets of muscles for the front and back movement. The more balanced use of leg muscles can be maintained for long hours of spinning. The treadle design also allows for a relaxed back position — you can sit squarely facing the wheel, even using both feet on the treadle for a more natural body position. This can help avoid the lower back pains that often afflict production spinners.

Softness and speed. The spinning method described in my *Spinning for Softness and Speed* is ideally suited for use with a Louet wheel, and is much easier to do on a Louet, with power on the bobbin and brake on the flyer, than on other single-belt wheels having power on the flyer and the brake on the bobbin.

The only adjustment you ever have to make on your Louet is the brake screw. It should be adjusted to give just the right amount of pull-in on the yarn for this one-handed, soft-spinning technique, so that the wheel can do all the work.

The Level-Wind Flyer and Bobbin
(The WooLee Winder)

There is a level-wind flyer and bobbin (called a WooLee Winder) that winds the yarn automatically onto the bobbin as you spin, and does not require you to stop and change hooks. It is available, as an accessory head for the Louet spinning wheel, from Robert Lee (see "Sources"). This attachment works exceptionally well on the Louet, better than it would work on a wheel with a Saxony-type treadle or a wheel that did not have the effortless treadle action of the Louet. Its bobbin has the same reversible feature as the regular Louet bobbins, allowing you the option of two different drive speeds.

Successful Entrepreneurs

Entrepreneur: *One who undertakes to start and conduct an enterprise or business, usually assuming full control and risk.*

HERE, PROVING THAT WOOL can indeed be turned into a cottage industry, are nineteen examples of wool-based businesses. The entrepreneurs described on the following pages show that a wool-based cottage industry need not be in any particular location, that the business can involve one person or several, and that the end result may be a single, logical product or a variety of unexpected by-products. Some of the people described here illustrate how a business can end up quite differently from what was first anticipated, and that the route to success will have a few roadblocks. But there is one thing these businesses all have in common: one way or another, they've all found a way to bring in income from wool.

ALICE IN WONDERLAND

ALICE STOUGH

WEST VIRGINIA

Alice Stough lives with her husband Lee and their three children on a 111-acre hilltop farm. Starting with Suffolk and Hampshire sheep, they have been crossing with Romney, aiming for all Romney-type fleeces, and are now getting about fifty shades of black, brown, and gray.

The fleeces are washed and hand-carded for spinning. For thirteen years, Alice has been using her yarn to knit sweaters, scarves, and ponchos, and to crochet large blankets. She has also recently been working with some locally raised mohair.

Lee does all the shearing and raises organic food for the sheep as well as for the family. The couple preserves most of their own food and home-teach their children, striving to be as self-sufficient as possible.

CERRO MOJINO WOOLWORKS
CONNIE AND SAM TAYLOR
NEW MEXICO

Sam and Connie run a carding business and a fifty-ewe flock on 60 waterless, powerless, serviceless acres in northern New Mexico. It is in a pinion-juniper-sagebrush belt that was previously declared uninhabitable by the U.S. government. There is no water (1200 feet down maybe, or 15 miles to haul), no electricity ($30,000 to bring in), no mail (15 miles away), and no phone.

Connie Taylor, of Cerro Mojino Woolworks, with lamb.

After assessing (and ignoring) all of the negative aspects of such a location, Sam and Connie fenced and revegetated 60 acres with hardy luna pubescent grass, using extensive cross fencing for "cell" grazing. Gradually the house, studio, and barns were built. Water is collected from all roof surfaces into storage tanks and ponds for the sheep. This provides for sheep, wool scouring on a small scale, and the household. Once or twice a year it becomes necessary to haul water in 270-gallon hauling tanks on their truck.

A Patrick Green Cottage Industry carder has been processing wool for Connie and Sam since 1984. Connie buys 2 tons of choice wool and 700 pounds of mohair each year for dyed wool/mohair blends to sell to spinners, and she does some custom carding. An amp meter assures the most efficient use of the carder. Most electrical needs are met from a battery-storage system charged by a 100-watt array of solar panels and a small 200-watt Winco Wincharger (wind-powered generator).

C. LEMAR
CHRISTINE LEMAR
WISCONSIN

Christine LeMar has been spinning since 1969, and started selling a few years later. At one time she offered a very wide range of yarn types,

Christine LeMar removing yarns from the dyepot.

Kay does the color planning and mixing for the exotic, multicolored rovings and batts.

with over a dozen different kinds on her sample card. She has now narrowed this down to two kinds of lumpy singles yarns that sell very well both retail and wholesale.

Her two types of dyed yarn are made in quite different ways. One yarn is spun and space-dyed afterward with Cushing or another synthetic dye. The other type is dyed as fleece with vegetable dyes, then processed with the wool picker and drum carder before spinning.

While Christine does some direct sales from her studio, she relies on a mail-order business to offset the economic slumps that occur in her area.

Much of her spinning is done on an electric bulk spinner made by her father, Sam Noto (shown in *Spinning and Weaving with Wool*). He made this spinner for Christine so that she could continue her spinning when she was recovering from an auto accident. She still uses it, finding it most suitable to the types of yarn that she now produces.

Custom Colors
Kay and Joe Fielding
Nevada

Kay and Joe are partners in a business offering multicolored spinning fibers and yarns. They specialize in soft wools suitable for clothing, and blends of wool/mohair, silk/mohair, and wool/silk/mohair, with more blends always being tested. Solid colors are offered to match the multicolors for greater design possibilities.

Living in the Desert Southwest has made them aware of the importance of cotton blends. The most popular are the cotton/silk known as "Pearls" and the "Cultured Pearls," which are cotton/

ramie, cotton/silk/rayon, and cotton/rayon. These are offered in soft, fluffy, easy-spinning batts featuring many colors per batt, blended for rapid color changes.

Kay does all the color planning and dyeing of fibers, while Joe runs the Jumbo Pat Green carder that he calls the "Mastercarder." They also sell spinning and weaving equipment and teach classes, advertise in magazines, and attend several spinning conferences a year. Business is by mail order, both wholesale and retail.

DEB MENZ
WISCONSIN

Deb Menz produces yarn, and she says she can easily sell all of it, mainly by selling through craft fairs and by mail, with some wholesaling to shops. She especially enjoys selling directly to customers, as that gives her a chance to explain how to use handspun and results in satisfied customers who reorder. She buys mainly New Zealand fleeces because she finds the local fleeces have too much vegetable matter.

Deb Menz, spinning natural-color yarn from New Zealand fleeces.

PHOTOGRAPH BY DAVID DENNIS

Deb washes all her fleeces and spins natural-color yarns as well as yarn from fleeces dyed with Ciba/ Kiton acid dyes. She usually blends several dye lots together in a wool picker, then uses a drum carder to prepare them for spinning.

Deb's skill at color blending has involved her in writing articles for *Color Trends* and teaching drum-carder color-blending at national spinning and weaving conferences.

GREEN MOUNTAIN SPINNERY
DAVID RITCHIE, CLAIRE WILSON, AND LIBBY MILLS
VERMONT

In December of 1981, the Green Mountain Spinnery began producing wool yarns from local New England fleece, with the distinction of being one of the smallest complete wool-processing mills in the country.

The Spinnery sends white wool out for scouring, but does the washing of all its dark wool right at the mill. Small equipment is used; production is scaled at approximately 300 pounds of raw wool per week. The mill sells yarns of high quality, both wholesale and retail, at a price competitive with mass-produced yarn.

The Spinnery will buy good-quality wool, paying about one third more than wool-pool prices for white wool, but pays more for good dark wool. The clean wool that is purchased must be mostly free of second cuts, 2½- to 5-inch staple, stored in burlap bags, and of medium grade (about 50s count). The price paid will depend on quality and quantity. For details, phone (802) 387-4528, or, if you want to sell, send fleece samples to Box 54, Putney, Vermont 05346; state the breed of sheep, staple length, estimated number of pounds, means of storage, name of the shearer, and date of shearing.

If you want custom spinning of your own wool, which includes scouring, picking, carding, spinning, and skeining, the mill requires a minimum quantity of 100 pounds of raw fleece. For custom scouring only, the minimum is 25 pounds of one color; for custom carding, which includes scouring, picking, and carding the minimum is 100 pounds. Send an SASE for prices. Another arrangement can be an exchange of fleece for yarn, in which case the wool price is determined as though the mill were buying outright. The sheep breeder can then apply that price to the purchase of Green Mountain Spinnery yarn at a discount.

The van Stralens' son Wouter at a Hilltop Wools shearing day.

HILLTOP WOOLS
TRUDY AND JAN VAN STRALEN
ONTARIO

Trudy's shop, open Fridays and Saturdays only, stocks fleece, weaving yarn, dyes, books, shuttles and looms, spinning wheels, and her own handspun, hand-dyed, and handwoven garments. Much of her weaving combines her handspun yarn with dyed, unspun locks of long wool.

The long-wool, soft-spun yarns that Trudy spins are much in demand for knitting, particularly for soft shawls. Some of these yarns are natural sheep colors, others have been dyed in the fleece with vegetable dyes. Because of her long experience in vegetable dyeing in large quantity, her expertise is in demand, so she teaches volume dyeing at spinning and weaving conferences across the country. Occasional workshops and private lessons are also given at the shop.

The van Stralen farm raises Coopworth and Lincoln sheep and crosses of the two breeds; van Stralens sell breeding stock, both white and dark sheep.

INDIAN SPRINGS FARM
AVELENE AND JIM McCAUL
MISSOURI

Avelene McCaul's shop is closed from the first of December through March because of winter weather and lambing season. The rest of the year she sells her natural-color handspun and vegetable-dyed handspun (retail only) plus spinning and weaving supplies and some of her dark fleeces.

A Great Pyrenees guard dog protects Avelene's herd of black sheep, kept exclusively for spinning wools. She uses a Lincoln-Coopworth ram and mostly Border Leicester ewes. Some fleeces are sold on Wool Day, the first week of May, but most are reserved for her own spinning.

Avelene McCaul at historic Indian Springs Farm.

Part of the attraction of her business is the historic environment. Indian Springs is an old plantation, with many of the original log cabins still intact. The McCauls have restored the house, also made of logs, constructing a modern kitchen but leaving the rest much as it would have been when it was first built. They have owned it for eighteen years, but were away for about five years of that time, coming back to raise sheep and really restore the farm. The old slave kitchen is now repaired and used as a dye house for the vegetable dyeing and classes. The other old buildings are being reconstructed, one by one, for uses connected with wool. The original hard bricks, hand made by slaves, are still there and can be used in the restoration.

JONES SHEEP FARM
MARILYN AND GARY JONES
KANSAS

The Jones Sheep Farm, with 225 head, has one of the largest black-sheep flocks in the United States. The Joneses have developed their

A yearling at Jones Sheep Farm, which specializes in black sheep breeds.

own strain of black sheep, combining Border Leicester, Lincoln, Cotswold, Romney, Corriedale, and Karakul, with 95 percent black-lamb crop. The wool is medium to coarse grade, 6-inch staple, with light grease and light shrinkage. They also keep distinct breeds, and sell the wool of about twenty different breeds at the farm or by mail, with a minimum order of 5 pounds per breed-fleece.

The most wanted fleeces by breed have been in descending order of popularity: Romney/Corriedale, colored crossbreed, Corriedale, Karakul, the farm's own spinning crossbreed, and Cotswold. Fleeces are all skirted and the skirtings sold to the local wool market.

In addition to selling wool and breeding stock, they sell natural-color pelts tanned at Bucks County Fur Products (see "Sources").

The farm offers summer classes in spinning that draw spinners from many parts of the country. In addition, there are occasional classes in cheese-making, using milk from goats kept at the farm primarily to supply milk for orphan lambs.

The Joneses' own book *Breeds of Sheep*, is sold by mail (see "Sources").

Luisa Gelenter, La Lana Wools.

LA LANA WOOLS
LUISA GELENTER
NEW MEXICO

Luisa Gelenter started out in business in 1973 with a partner, selling only handspun, vegetable-dyed yarns. Her partner dropped out of the business, but Luisa is still going and has diversified considerably in the meantime. She still uses only vegetable dyes, no chemical ones, but sells in quite a few forms: carded rainbow-dyed batts for other spinners and feltmakers, dyed silk yarn, dyed handspun wool, dyed kid mohair handspun, heavily textured handspun yarns, and dyed homespun-type yarn.

In addition to her long-standing mail-order business, Luisa has now opened a small retail store, featuring all of her products as well as vegetable-dye materials, mordants, and warp yarns for weavers.

MUNROE WOOL COMPANY
JOHN AND MARJORIE MUNROE
WASHINGTON

The Munroes have a lot of wool, but only three sheep, which they use as lawn mowers. They purchase local wool for the wool-filled comforters that have a ready sale without paid advertising. One good source of orders is a prestigious bed-and-breakfast resort that uses these comforters and lets the guest know where to buy them.

Marjorie's Cottage Industry carder has been preparing the wool comforter/quilt batts since 1982, as well as doing custom carding for spinners. In 1989, John retired from his job at a local radio station and wanted to join his wife's full-time carding efforts, so they purchased a second Cottage Industry carder, a Jumbo that could process fine wools and exotics and produce center-pull balls, as well as loose roving and large batts. This required the construction of a larger workshop. This shop was barely done when they had a disastrous house fire and had to live in the shop with their carders for several months while rebuilding their home. Now all is back to normal, with the industrious couple working side by side at their "his-and-hers" carders.

THE RIVER FARM
PRISCILLA BLOSSER-RAINEY AND JERRY RAINEY
VIRGINIA

The River Farm is famous for its weekend spinning and dyeing workshops, which are held all summer long at this sheep farm in the Shenandoah Valley. Camping facilities make it possible for students to come from distant places. There are also occasional workshops on flock management, as well as private lessons on flock management and spinning.

The Corriedale and Corriedale crosses raised at The River Farm are kept under sheepcovers all year, resulting in exceptionally clean fleeces, which are well skirted for sale to spinners at the farm or by mail. Prices include the cost of UPS shipping. In addition to white wool and dark wool, the couple sells breeding stock, handspun yarn, spinning and weaving supplies.

Priscilla keeps in touch with customers by sending out schedules and brochures to people on the mailing list she has built up, as well as doing extensive magazine advertising and taking booths at craft fairs and weaving conferences. She has been in business at this location since 1973.

Spinner's Hill
Lisa Ann Merian
New York

Lisa Ann started her shop in 1981, while she was still in high school. By 1983 she was able to buy a Cottage Industry carder, and two years later needed the powered wool picker to keep up with the volume of business.

With 375 sheep and 25 angora goats on her family's farm, there is an abundance of wool, so she can use the very best for spinning fibers and the lesser quality for quilt and felting batts. In addition to selling carded fibers, she finds a ready market for dyed wool/mohair blends direct from the picker, which appeal to spinners for both appearance and price.

Spinner's Hill shop sells spinning wheels, dyes, yarn, fibers, and looms, as well as takes in custom carding. Lisa Ann markets her fibers at many sheep and wool festivals from May through November. Helping with the "hothouse lamb" marketing extends to April. The festivals are mostly on weekends, so midweek in the summer is busy with wool washing, dyeing, and carding; and the mail-order business is steady all through the year.

Spring Creek Farm
Judy Lewman
Minnesota

The first year of mail-order business at Spring Creek Farm turned a five-figure gross and a small profit. By the second year, sales had tripled. After fifteen years of business from its forty-acre sheep farm, Spring Creek can boast that its logo, a 200-year-old woodcut of a Border Leicester sheep, is one of the most widely known logos in the business.

Judy Lewman markets her own Border Leicester fleeces and selected top-quality fleeces from a few local growers. She says the farm has been able to accept wool from only about 15 percent of the flocks inspected. To get the quality needed, it has been necessary to import the rest of the wool from New Zealand. In addition to fleeces, Spring

Creek Farm also sells breeding stock, books, yarn, fibers, and spinning and weaving equipment, including Schacht looms and Louet wheels.

To reach customers, Judy advertises in twenty publications, with some display ads but primarily classified ads. Her brochure cost is kept down with simple illustrations and a separate page for prices. The brochure offers "top quality products at a fair price." Spring Creek Farm strives to provide prompt, personal service, expert advice when needed, and merchandise in stock for immediate shipment.

SPRINGWATER SPINOFFS

KATHLEEN SULLIVAN

OREGON

Kathleen Sullivan with part of her flock.

Kathy and her family live on a 46-acre farm, where they have a large Angora rabbitry with all four breeds, and also raise both white and colored angora goats.

A spinner and weaver since the early 1970s, Kathy started her custom-carding service in response to a dire need for a facility that could prepare bunny, mohair, and exotic blends. Using two custom-designed Patrick Green carders for fine and exotic fibers, she does a large volume of specialty fiber carding, most of which could not be handled on large mill machinery.

Kathy and her husband, Tim, are currently increasing the number of colored Angora goats in their herd, although they will continue to keep about fifty white ones. They sell breeding stock from both rabbits and goats.

In addition to processing fiber blends of her own creation for spinners, Kathy offers handspun yarn from her own fibers, hand dyed in unique color patterns, as well as raw fibers from the goats and rabbits. She teaches many workshops related to exotic fibers, animal management, and business-related issues for craftspeople.

WOODLAND WOOLWORKS

MELDA AND CHARLIE MONTGOMERY

OREGON

Woodland Woolworks produces innovative, high-quality fiber products for handspinners, using 100 percent wool and wool blends in natu-

Melda has a plexiglass shield and a suction unit above her carder that make it unnecessary to wear a dust mask as protection against dust and fine, airborne fibers.

ral and dyed colors. With both white and natural-colored Lincoln, Corriedale, and Romney sheep, they have for twelve years bred for the colors and wool qualities desired by spinners, using sheep coats to guard fleeces against weathering and contamination.

Melda is an accomplished spinner, knitter, and weaver, so is well-qualified to create unique products and advise her customers. She always keeps in mind that quality and customer satisfaction are the cornerstones of a successful business.

Woodland Woolworks started as a part-time family operation, and now includes several employees as the business continually grows and develops new products and services. One most attractive specialty is the rainbow roving of dyed wool and mohair, done in several color ranges.

Wool and Feathers
Gisela Gminder
Vermont

Gisela Gminder arrived in Vermont via Germany, Pasadena, and Boston. While skiing in Vermont, she was lured by the attractions of country living and decided to buy a rundown farm, where she started raising sheep. She began selling yarn, mittens, wool comforters, and Kaunakes vests (*kaunakes* is ancient Greek for "making warm cloth from sheep's wool") from the tailgate of her pickup truck, going to craft fairs and general stores.

Gisela's first business venture was a shop in Winooski, with a partner. The commute provided to be difficult in the winter months, so the next step was a Wool and Feathers shop in the charming village of Stowe. Starting with a small space, Gisela eventually bought a historic home in the downtown area to house the shop.

Gisela's main product is still yarn from local sheep, but the selection is supplemented by mohairs, silks, linen, and alpaca. Handcrafted rugs, sweaters, and other fine fibercrafts are offered for sale along with looms and weaving supplies, spinning wheels, and her own fleeces. The most recent addition is a meat license; with two large freezers below the shop, she can now sell single cuts of meat instead of just the customary whole lamb. Freezer lambs can also be ordered and picked up all cut and wrapped.

In addition, spinning, weaving, knitting, and felting classes are held regularly in the shop.

WOOLGATHERINGS
SANDY SITZMAN
OREGON

Oregon has more llamas than any other state, and some of these are at Sandy Sitzman's farm, where they share their pasture with her flock of black sheep; all are being raised for their fiber production. Sandy clips her llamas every 12 to 18 months, and gets from 3 to 5 pounds of 6-inch staple per fleece. To get yarn with increased springiness, sheep's wool is blended with the llama, then carded on a Cottage Industry carder. Since Sandy is a weaver, she uses much of this blended fiber to spin for her own woven items, or sells it in the form of handspun — soft, medium weight, one

Lydia the llama, with sheep.

ply. Selling dyed fleece and handspun, dyed yarn has led to the blending and carding of dyed wools for her spinner customers, and this service is growing in popularity. One interesting specialty is the complete processing for other weavers. Sandy washes fleeces, dyes, picks, cards and blends, and then spins into weaving yarn, all to the customer's specifications.

WOOLY HILL FARM
GREG PAHL AND NANCY LOW
VERMONT

As a result of proper care and skillful marketing, the purebred Corriedale and Dorset fleeces from Wooly Hill Farm sold out to handspinners within two weeks of shearing, at between $3.00 and $4.50 a pound (1983-84 prices). Much of the following year's clip was also sold in advance.

About a third of the farm's income from sheep is from the sale of wool and handspun yarn, and another third from the sale of breeding stock. The remainder is generated by freezer lambs, pelts, and awards from fairs. Additional income comes from an extensive wood-lot operation (firewood and sawlogs) undertaken to clear more pasture land.

After starting their sheep venture in 1979, with no experience, Greg and Nancy signed up for all the sheep seminars that were available, joined the Vermont Sheep Breeders Association, and participated in the Vermont Sheep Project, an educational program on sheep-management skills. As of 1985, Greg has served on the board of directors of both the Vermont Ram Test and the Vermont Sheep Breeders Association.

By direct marketing of their wool and their lambs, and helped by awards at local and regional fairs, Greg and Nancy have not had to rely on wool pools and lamb pools, and have been pleased with the improved prices for their products.

Questions and Answers

Business Questions

Q. *I live in a remote area. How can I establish a business?*

A. Decide what business, and advertise to more populated areas. A mail-order business is ideal for an isolated community, as long as there is a post office nearby. Start small and work up.

Q. *How will I know what to charge for yarn, yardage, or garments?*

A. Notice what is being charged for comparable items. There are two ways to look at it: What is it worth? What can you get for it where it is being sold? It is important not to price an item too high for the location in which it is being sold. If you do, you are only pricing it, not selling it. For more information see my book *Handspinners Guide to Selling.*

Q. *I know of one person who is attracting customers from a great distance, when they could be dealing with someone closer. She says the customers like her attitude. Is attitude that important?*

A. Attitude really does make a difference. There is a knack to getting along with people, and not everyone has this as a natural ability. However, it can be cultivated. Among the qualities needed are a fairly even disposition, a bit of tact, a willingness to meet your customer halfway (or more), and, in particular, a sense of humor. A firmness about payment after invoicing (or payment in advance if that is your policy) must be tempered with a sufficiently friendly attitude so that the customer does not become offended. No matter how choice your merchandise, the competition can woo away your customer by showing thoughtfulness and good humor, if you lack these traits.

Q. *What about exotic fibers? Can I sell mohair from Angora goats, or Angora rabbit hair, or llama wool?*

A. The mohair from Angora goats is quite popular and brings a good price if it is of good quality and clean. Angora rabbit fur is a good crop to raise, and is usually spun without carding. Llamas also are not difficult to raise, but they are very expensive animals and do not grow a very heavy crop of wool to sell.

Q. *How can I be sure I can make money with a Cottage Industry carder?*

A. Making money is not automatic. A businesslike attitude is important, and diversification keeps money coming in from a variety of sources. You need to do selective advertising and have a good descriptive brochure detailing what you have to offer. Make it easy and pleasant for customers to do business with you, and do a careful job. When shipping carded wool, package it tidily with a legible label.

Q. *There is a dire need for a sheltered workshop for the handicapped in our area. What sort of wool work would fit in with the capabilities of these people, and is there a market for their products?*

A. Working with wool is pleasant, and ideal for a sheltered workshop. At one such workshop, in Langley, British Columbia, workers take wool from the raw state to finished articles, washing, dyeing, then spinning and weaving horse blankets and other items. They also do custom weaving, and organizers say there is more demand than they can fill. Some wool is purchased, some is donated. The shop had not been operating long when it became necessary to expand the work area and set up a more efficient dye shop in order to increase the output.

Woolcraft Questions

Buying, Storing, and Sorting Wool

Q. *Where can I buy good raw wool?*

A. Try to locate wool in your own area, to save postage. Find out the local wool price, and offer a better price for clean, nicely sheared and skirted fleeces. If you cannot locate wool in your area, look in the ads in *The Black Sheep Newsletter, SpinOff,* and other fiber publications.

Q. *I bought a fleece that has a very tender staple and breaks easily. What causes this, and how can I use this wool?*

A. Tenderness in a fleece could be caused by a sheep's illness, nutritional deficiency, lack of water for an extended period, a sudden change of pasture or feed, a difficult lambing, or severe internal parasites. If the wool is clean enough, try spinning it directly from the fleece, as this will minimize breaking. Breakage during carding will not lessen its usefulness for handmade felt or for quilt batts.

Q. *I would like to see some prime-quality handspinning wool to compare to my own wool. Where can I get samples to show me what quality I should try to work for?*

A. Look in *SpinOff* or in *Handwoven,* and write to some of the advertisers who offer fleece samples for a specified price. Do not ask for free samples, and send a self-addressed, stamped envelope when writing to individuals for information. This courtesy is appreciated.

Q. *How should I store wool in hot climates? In damp climates?*

A. For raw wool, I suggest large, double-thickness paper bags, like feed bags. In damp climates, these could be enclosed in large plastic bags. Wooden crates, plastic- or paper-lined, are also good.

Q. *What is the difference between* wool grading *and* wool sorting?

A. Grading pertains to the variations between different fleeces, mainly according to the fineness of the wool, which changes noticeably between breed types. Wool sorting has to do with the variations between wool types and quality within each fleece. A fleece is sorted for fineness, staple length, crimp, tenderness, contamination, color, density, and softness. For commercial purposes, uniformity of wool within a fleece is best because it requires less sorting time.

Felting and Carding

Q. *Why is feltmaking so appealing to craftsmen?*

A. It is a creative craft, allowing for a maximum of decoration to be incorporated into the actual felt, plus surface ornamentation afterward. It can be almost as versatile as yardage if well done, and can contribute parts to be worked into unique and one-of-a-kind garments or decorative objects. A great attraction, if you can work it into your enterprise, is that you can generate income from otherwise wasted wool. After the carding drums on the Cottage Industry carder have been cleaned, for instance, some of the fibers removed from the drums, the short wool fibers that fall beneath the carder, and the belly wool and stained tags, when washed and carded, all can go into felt.

Q. *How does feltmaking fit into a wool-based cottage industry?*

A. It is good as one facet, excellent if part of a total picture. Feltmaking is hard work and can take too much time unless you can develop a system that works in your situation. You do need a space to work in, where water used in felting can drain away, and boiling or near-boiling water can be used without damaging the surroundings. There are some people who specialize in feltmaking and do a good job of it.

Q. *The Cottage Industry carder shown in the book* Spinning for Softness and Speed *looks different from ones I've seen recently. What is different?*

A. The machine shown in that book, depending on whether first or second printing, was a recent ancestor of the current machines. The newer ones are more sophisticated, with a better flycomb and a much larger storage roll, which makes a larger batt. Some of the current models not only make a continuous roving (sliver) but wind it automatically into a center-pull ball for spinning.

Q. *I want to develop a cottage-industry carding business, but do not have electricity. Do you have any suggestions?*

A. There is a Cottage Industry carder in New Mexico that is being operated without electricity. Connie Taylor of Cerro Mojino Woolworks has a 200-watt Winco windcharger and three 35-watt photovoltaic panels to generate electricity. The storage bank is twenty-four 185-amp-hour 6-

volt batteries salvaged from A.T.&T. Her half-horsepower motor on the carder draws 40 amps maximum, and she uses it for 42 hours of carding per month, to card the wool from her forty-five spinning-wool ewes, and the wool of local farm flocks (see page 153).

Q. *Does the Cottage Industry carder do a better job of carding than a large mill carder?*

A. I feel that it does a better job for *handcraft* purposes, causing less damage to the fibers while preserving the special attributes of the different wool types. At the same time it provides more control over the resulting batt or roving (sliver).

Q. *What is the estimated life of the teeth on the Cottage Industry carder?*

A. If used six days a week, twelve hours a day, the carder should not need sharpening for at least five years. The life span of the teeth is shortened if you damage the cloth by allowing hard objects to go through with the wool. The cloth used is commercial carding cloth, the kind used in Britain by the wool trade.

Washing

Q. *Isn't soap better than detergent for wool washing?*

A. Detergent rinses out more easily, and leaves less film on the wool.

Q. *My family objects to the strong odor when I wash large quantities of wool for processing. Is there a solution to this smell?*

A. Indoors, good ventilation will quickly remove this smell. In good weather, do your washing outdoors. Tell your family that if you work it right, the odor of washing wool is the smell of gold.

Q. *If I want to knit a sweater with wool in the grease, can I just wash the wool in cold water to leave in the lanolin?*

A. Yes. After spinning, wash the yarn in cool water to set the twist as much as possible before knitting, or spin in the grease and then wash the yarn in cool water. Wash the finished sweater in cool water only.

Q. *How can I solve the problem of washing wool in hard water?*

A. Use water softener and a little washing soda as necessary. Be glad you have hard water; it is better for your health.

Spinning and Dyeing

Q. *How many pounds of yarn can be spun in an hour?*

A. Wow, what a question. That depends on so many things: the size of the yarn being spun, the quality and preparation of the wool, the efficiency of the spinning wheel, and the skill and experience of the spinner. With a good wheel, well-carded wool, and medium-size yarn, a rough estimate might be 3 pounds an hour.

Q. *Is mohair good for dyeing?*

A. Mohair is beautiful when dyed, thanks to its high luster.

Quilting Batts

Q. *Do people really use wool batts inside quilts? All I ever see advertised are synthetic battings.*

A. Wool batts are the traditional stuffing for quilts and comforters and preferred by anyone who has used a quilt containing wool. Modern substitutes are convenient, but not necessarily satisfying. For easy care, quilt a wool batt into a plain cotton envelope and slide the pieced quilt over it, like a huge pillow slip. The outer quilt can be washed easily, without the need to wash the inner wool batting.

Classes

Q. *Are there college courses that teach wool-working as a profession?*

A. I know of none. Textile and fiber courses at the college level are not too helpful when it comes to earning a living in the real world. Build on your own experience, read everything available, talk to those who are ahead of you in your field, and learn from your mistakes.

Sheep Questions

Facts about Sheep

Q. *Which country has the most sheep?*

A. The 1981 census showed the number of sheep in the Soviet Union to have reached 147 million, making that the largest sheep population in the world. The U.S.S.R. has a wide variety of climate conditions and 61 different breeds of sheep, including 24 fine-wool breeds, 20 semi-fine, 3 semi-coarse, and 14 coarse. The coarse and semi-coarse breeds are kept for mutton and to provide pelts for coats.

Q. *I'm a vegetarian. Can't sheep be raised just for wool?*

A. Hardly. If sheep were not raised for meat, commercial sheepraising would cease, and the supply of wool would dwindle and virtually disappear. All serious users of wool should actively encourage consumption of lamb and mutton to insure a future supply of wool.

Q. *If wool is so good for keeping people warm, don't sheep suffer in hot weather?*

A. In hot climates, wool keeps the sheep cool. In the hottest Australian season, wool temperature at the tip of the staple may be 180° F., but the skin temperature of the sheep will be only 107° F. (3 degrees hotter than their body temperature).

Buying Sheep

Q. *Older ewes are often sold at auction at ridiculously low prices. Would buying several of these ewes be a good way to start a flock at low cost?*

A. When you buy cull ewes at an auction, you do not have a chance to observe the flock they come from or to note signs of foot problems or disease. Buying old ewes directly from the farm would be safer.

Q. *What would be the best time of year for me to start a small flock by buying two or more ewes?*

A. You will not need to buy a ram the first year, if you get bred ewes in the fall, when the ewes will have grown enough wool for you to judge the quality of their fleece. You might be better off buying sheep that are two or three years old, since yearlings may not be as good mothers. An old ewe may be a good buy if she is in good health.

Q. *When I'm buying a sheep, can I tell its age by looking at its teeth?*

A. Yes. For a sheep up to about four years old, you can tell the age by the *number* of teeth. After that, estimate the age by the *condition* of the teeth. The term *solid mouth* describes an adult sheep with all its permanent teeth in place and fitting solidly together. A sheep with teeth in this condition would be about four years old (older if it has been on good pasture). *Spreaders* are older sheep with teeth that show wear and that are narrower, with more of the undergum portion of the teeth moved into the gums. Older sheep with some teeth missing are called *broken mouth*. If an old ewe is down to one or two loose teeth, pull these out with pliers. The gums will harden so that she can eat grass more efficiently than she could with only a couple of teeth.

Breeding

Q. *Can you define the terms purebred, grade, and scrub?*

A. A sheep whose parents belong to the same breed and are registered or eligible to be registered in the record books of a recognized breed association is called a purebred. A grade is one having the characteristics of a breed but no registration papers. A scrub is an animal of mixed or unknown breed, but the term is seldom used any more.

Q. *What, besides crossbreeding, can encourage out-of-season lambing?*

A. Longer days will increase the chances of ewes successfully rebreeding. The U.S. Sheep Experiment Station at Dubois, Idaho has been experimenting with housing ewes in barns with supplemental lighting, to encourage two lamb crops per year.

Q. *I have used my black ram for several years and kept many of his daughters. How can I locate another good dark ram so as to avoid excessive inbreeding?*

A. Advertise in *The Black Sheep Newsletter*. The classified ads are inexpensive and get good results, as this publication goes to many small-flock owners who also have this problem. You may be able to trade rams with someone else who has a good proven ram.

Q. *What can I cross with a meat breed such as Suffolk to obtain good spinning wool that will sell well?*

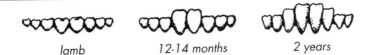

lamb   12-14 months   2 years

3 years   4 years

The approximate age of a sheep up to about four years old can be determined by counting its permanent teeth. At twelve to fourteen months, the two center milk teeth have been replaced by permanent teeth. Another pair of permanent teeth appears annually for the next three years.

After four years, the degree of wearing, or spreading, of teeth gives a rough indication of a sheep's age.

Annual wear after:

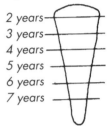

2 years
3 years
4 years
5 years
6 years
7 years

A. Crosses of meat breeds with either Merino or a long-wool breed could produce a different wool, but the criterion is the personal preference of the sheepraiser. Medium wools of a good length seem to be the favorite. To obtain a wool of 4- to 6-inch staple length, cross with one of the long-wool breeds such as Lincoln, Leicester, or Romney.

Q. *What could I cross with Merino or Rambouillet to obtain a salable spinning wool?*

A. Merino is now much more popular than in the past, so the production of pure Merino, if the fleece is kept clean and sheared carefully, could be profitable. If you want a longer fleece with less crimp, the Black and Coloured Sheep Breeders Association of Australia advises Merino owners to look for rams from one of the British long-wool breeds; the resulting progeny should produce a good spinning fleece. As with any crossbreeding, select the lambs you keep for the fleece type you want, and cull out those that do not meet your standards.

Shelter and Pasture

Q. *Can I keep sheep in hillside brush country?*

A. You might want Angora goats first; they are good brush clearers ahead of sheep. If you enjoy working with mohair, keep the goats and run sheep with them after they have cleared out much of the brush. Goats are browsers and eat leafy brush more than 10 inches high. Sheep are grazers and prefer to eat grass from ground level to about 6 inches high. They work well together, unless the goats have horns.

Q. *How large should a shelter be, to be practical for just a few sheep?*

A. An acceptable size would be about 12 square feet per sheep, if they will need to be in it for protection from bad weather.

Q. *Are any plants poisonous to sheep, and will sheep eat them?*

A. If short on forage, sheep may eat some of the many plants that are poisonous to them. Among these are black laurel, chokecherry, wild cherry, goldenrod, tansy ragwort, some ferns, death camas, heliotrope, locoweed, lupine, milkweed, spotted (poison) hemlock, water hemlock, St. Johnswort, foxglove, oleander, and privet. Poisonous garden plants are rhubarb, green potatoes, and potato sprouts. Poinsettias and English ivy, which are common houseplants, should be kept away from sheep.

Getting Rid of Ticks

Q. *How do you use rotenone to eliminate ticks? What kind of rotenone?*

A. You can order the 5 percent wettable powder rotenone (usually 5-pound bags) from Sheepman Supply Company (see "Sources"). Use 8 ounces to 100 gallons of water (1½ ounces to a 20-gallon garbage can) for either dipping the lambs or sloshing on the adults. Mix the powder to a paste in a small amount of water, then add it to the larger quantity of water. If sheep have any fleece, you may need to add a small squirt of dishwashing detergent to make the liquid more penetrating. It is most effective when applied right after shearing. With the sheep on its back, slosh the dip on its neck, chest, and belly. Let the sheep stand up, then slosh the dip over its top from head to tail. Most tick eggs will have been eliminated in shearing, but if many are left on the sheep, you may need to apply rotenone again twenty-four days later to get those that hatch. If dusting instead of using liquid, use 1.5 percent garden dust — about 2 ounces per sheep. Rotenone is safe for both ewes and lambs right up to the time of slaughter.

Mulesing

Q. *What is a mulesing operation? We don't hear about it in the U.S.*

A. Mulesing is an operation that is done on Merinos in some countries to remove sagging skin wrinkles from the breech, making the skin fit tightly over the hindquarters. The elimination of these skin folds (so prevalent on Merinos) can almost prevent fly strike problems there. Not enough Merinos are raised in the U.S. to make it a common procedure.

Glossary

ARTIFICIAL SELECTION. See *Selection.*

BATT. A mass of carded fibers from a carding machine.

BELLY WOOL. Wool grown on the sheep's belly, usually more tangled with vegetable matter and dirt than other wool, uneven in grade, and less desirable. Belly wool should be removed in skirting.

BLOOM. A particular brightness on the cut side of a shorn fleece, resulting from a healthy sheep's being shorn in the spring, when the yolk is fresh and not yet hardened on the wool by warm weather.

BRAID. Long, coarse wool from luster-wool breeds.

BREAK. A weakness in fiber at a certain point in the staple, usually caused by the sheep's illness or malnutrition, or by harsh weather. A fleece with breaks is sometimes called *tender* by spinners (although commercially "tender" refers to generally weak fibers).

BRITCH. The lower hindquarters of a sheep, or the wool from this area. Of lower quality than the rest of the fleece, britch wool should be removed in skirting if it is badly stained or heavy with mud or manure.

BURRY WOOL. Wool with excessive vegetable matter, especially burrs, which have become so embedded in the wool that they are difficult to remove. Commercially, burry wool can include other vegetation such as leaves, twigs, and seeds.

CANARY STAINED WOOL. A yellow discoloration most often found in imported wools and said to be caused by hot and humid temperatures before shearing.

CARBONIZING. The commercial process of treating wool with sulfuric acid and then baking it, to destroy burrs and other vegetation.

CARDING. The opening up, straightening, and aerating of washed wool fibers before spinning.

CARPET WOOL. Long coarse wool with a count of 40 or less. The most prized of the carpet wools are from New Zealand or Australia.

CHARACTER. A commercial term referring to the evenness and uniformity of the crimp.

CLEAN WOOL. Usually a reference to its cleanliness from vegetation.

CLIP. The amount of wool in a single shearing of a sheep or a flock, state, or country, usually the annual shearing.

Conformation. A term referring to body type, the ideal being based on a number of judgments, primarily visual. Esminger's *Sheep and Wool Science*, in describing the ideal mutton breed, says it would include an animal of good size and depth, with width and compactness in the body, a short neck, deep chest, wide back and thick loin, length and levelness over the rump, large leg of mutton, straight legs, closeness to the ground, fleece of acceptable weight and quality, and a pink skin. Rams should show boldness, and ewes should be feminine.

Consignment. Turning over an item to a shop (or agent) with the understanding that you will get paid for the item when it is sold. The dealer takes a 40 percent commission (approximately) and passes the balance of the selling price to you. The item you consign remains your property, legally, until it is sold.

Cotty wool. Wool that has become matted or felted while on the sheep's back, making it difficult to separate the fibers without excessive breakage.

Count. A system of fleece classification that indicates the approximate diameter of the fibers on a scale of 100. A higher count indicates finer wool (see explanation in chapter 5).

Crimp. The natural waviness in wool fibers. Finer wools have more crimps per inch than medium wool, and medium wools have more crimps per inch than coarse wool. Crimp helps to give wool its natural elasticity and resilience.

Crossbreed. The sheep resulting from the crossing of two different breeds, or the wool from such a sheep.

Crutching. An Australian term for the practice of clipping the wool from the rear end of ewes prior to lambing or shearing. In the U.S. and Canada, the term is *tagging*.

Dead wool. Wool that has been pulled from a dead sheep, not a live sheep or even a slaughtered sheep. Dead or pulled wool is harder to spin because the fiber scales shrink when the animal dies.

Density. An indication of the number of wool fibers per inch on the sheep's body. Fine wools have greater density than coarser wools.

Direct selling. Selling retail directly to a customer.

Docking. Removal of a lamb's tail, usually done when the lamb is three days old or earlier.

Doggy wool. Wool that has a shallow crimp, some fibers being flatter than normal. Under a microscope, some localized enlargement of the fiber can be seen near the root. Doggy wool does *not* contain an excessive amount of yolk as is sometimes believed. This fault is most common in Merino wool.

Extract wool. A commercial term for wools obtained by carbonizing part-wool fabrics to remove the vegetable fibers. The resulting wool is shredded for blending with better wool for low-grade manufactured products.

FELTING. The matting together of wool fibers, usually by moisture, heat, pressure, and agitation. Careless washing can cause unintentional felting, while deliberate feltmaking is controlled.

FINE WOOL. A general term, usually, for wool of any of the fairly fine wool breeds: Merino, Rambouillet, or Debouillet. Commercially, it signifies the finest grade of wool according to the blood system.

FLEECE. Wool from a single sheep, either as it comes from the sheep or after it is rolled and tied. Or, wool still on the sheep.

FLUSHING. Supplementing the usual summer diet of the ewes with grain and/or better pasture prior to breeding.

FLY STRIKE. Maggots from blowfly eggs laid on wounded or manure-soiled areas of the sheep, on heavy skin folds, areas of fleece rot, or, sometimes, the area around the horns of horned breeds. Fly strike is not as easy to detect on dark sheep as on white, since the staining on the fleece caused by fly strike cannot be as readily seen on dark wool.

FROWSY WOOL. Dry, harsh, loose wool, uneven in crimp, and sometimes inelastic.

GRADING. The commercial classification of fleece into grades by count or class.

GREASE WOOL. Unwashed wool as it comes from the sheep, before any processing.

GUMMY WOOL. A classification used commercially to indicate wool on which the grease has solidified, making it hard to scour. Among handspinners, wool is considered gummy if it has been washed, but not thoroughly enough to get out all the stickiness. The term is also used to designate a fleece that has too much yolk.

HANDLE (HAND). A term that refers to the feel of wool: its resilience, its softness, and how pleasing it is to the touch.

HERITABILITY. The ability of a parent's characteristic to be passed on to the offspring.

HETEROSIS. Hybrid vigor, where the crossing of two breeds results in an animal with performance higher than the average of either breed.

HOGGETT. An Australian and New Zealand term for the first full fleece taken from a sheep, usually a sheep up to 15 months old.

HOMESPUN. A legal term to describe 1-ply mill yarn that is an imitation of handspun.

JACOB FLEECE. Fleece from the Jacob sheep, which is multicolored: black, white, and gray.

KEMP. Straight, opaque, coarse, inelastic fibers sometimes found in fleeces. Kemp fibers do not take a dye and do not resemble normal fleece fibers.

LAMB CREEP. An area with a constant supply of grain that lambs can enter and ewes cannot.

LAMB'S WOOL. Wool taken from a lamb not over seven months old, shorter and softer than that of successive shearings.

LANOLIN. Wool grease, sometimes called *yolk*. Lanolin is a secretion from the sebaceous glands that prevents the excessive drying of the fleece while on the sheep.

LOCK. A small group of fibers, about finger size, that cling together naturally. Some long-wool sheep have fleeces that hang in wavy locks.

LONG WOOL. Wool often up to 12 inches in length from coarse-wool sheep such as Lincoln, Leicester, and Cotswold.

LUSTER WOOLS. Wools that reflect light, partly due to the lack of serrations on the fibers. This wool sheen cannot be noted in single fibers, as it is the property of locks. The finest Merino is said to have *silver luster*. Long-wools such as Lincoln are known particularly as luster wools, having what is called *silk luster*. Romney wool is another long-luster type, having a *satin luster*. Mohair goat wool is said to have a *glass luster*.

MEDIUM WOOLS. Wools grading 50s to 62s, approximately.

MONO-MORDANTING. A dyeing procedure with the mordant in the dye bath, in contrast to premordanting, when you mordant before dyeing.

NEPS. Tiny bunches of entangled fibers noticed after carding, which can be caused by broken fibers, foreign matter, second cuts, or yolk that was not washed out sufficiently. Sometimes called *nibs, pills,* or *balls*.

NOILS. The short fibers combed out of the longer fibers in the combing process that follows carding in some commercial processing.

OFF-SORTS. The commercial term for the by-products of sorting such as second cuts, kempy patches, stained wool, dung tags.

PELT. The skin of a slaughtered sheep with the wool still on it.

PIECES. The Australian term for skirtings and other inferior wool removed from the fleece in sorting.

PRIME FLEECE (as used by spinners). The best quality wools — those that are well skirted and free of vegetable matter.

PROLIFICACY. A ewe's ability to produce multiple births.

PULLED WOOL. Wool taken from the pelts of slaughtered sheep in a commercial process. Pulled wool is not of as good quality as shorn wool due to slight enlargement at the fiber roots.

PURITY. A description of whether a wool is free of kemp, hairiness, or, in the case of white wool, dark fibers.

QUALITY. A commercial term that refers to the fineness of the wool fibers. In the handspinner's vocabulary, it has more to do with desirability and soundness.

RAW WOOL. Wool in the grease, as it comes from the sheep.

REPROCESSED WOOL. A legal term for wool that has been woven or felted into a wool product and then, without ever having been used in any way by a consumer, is returned to a fibrous state.

REUSED WOOL. A legal term for wool or reprocessed wool that has been spun, woven, knitted, or felted into a wool product and then, after being used in some way by the consumer, is returned to a fibrous state.

ROVING. A slightly twisted sliver or roll of wool, one of the final states of wool in mill processing prior to spinning. While roving is much thinner than sliver, the terms have come to be almost interchangeable in common usage, although they are not the same when used commercially.

SCOURING. Commercial washing to remove dirt, grease, and foreign matter from grease wool.

SECOND CUTS. Short snips of wool resulting from cutting the same wool fibers twice in shearing. Also called *double-cuts* and *fribs*.

SELECTION. Natural selection is the survival of the fittest. Artificial selection is the deliberate culling out and keeping of what the sheepraiser considers the best.

SHEARING. The removal of the wool from live sheep by means of powered clippers or hand shears.

SHEARLINGS. The pelts of slaughtered sheep having wool growth of about ¼ to 1 inch. The term is used for pelts before or after tanning.

SHORTS. Locks or bits of wool that drop out while sheared fleece is being sorted.

SHRINKAGE. The amount of weight lost during the commercial scouring and carbonizing of wool fleece.

SKIRTING. The removal of the edges of the whole shorn fleece to discard or set aside the undesirable portions.

SLIVER. A continuous, thick strand of scoured and carded wool, often called *roving* by spinners, although roving actually comes from a later process in manufacture.

SORTING. In commercial usage, the separation of the various qualities of wool in individual fleeces.

SOUND WOOL. Fleece with strong fibers and no breaks or weak tips.

STAPLE. Naturally formed locks, tufts, or clusters of wool fibers in shorn wool. Staples are joined by crossfibers, which bind the fleece together. Commercially, staple means wool that averages at least 2½ inches long.

SUB-ANAL LEATHERPATCH. A small, black, triangular, leathery patch below the anus in Suffolk sheep and some Suffolk crosses. This is a valuable characteristic in these sheep because the smooth surface discourages excretions from sticking to the wool and helps keep the wool dry in that area, greatly lowering the incidence of fly strike.

Suint. Sheep sweat, which is present in grease wool and can be easily washed out.

Tagging. The cutting or shearing off of dung locks prior to lambing or shearing. Also called *crutching.*

Tags. Large clumps of britch wool that are heavy with dung and should be removed in skirting.

Tender wool. Wool fiber that is weak at one or more places along its length. It is said to have a break if weak at only one place.

Tippy wool. Weathered wool with hardened grease and dirt at the tips, which break off during processing.

Top. A continuous strand of combed wool with fibers parallel, previously scoured and carded, then processed to remove shorter fibers. It is used for worsted yarn.

Tying a fleece. Using paper cord to tie rolled wool, cut side out, into a bundle. Other kinds of twine will contaminate the fleece.

Vegetable matter. Any kind of burr, seed, chaff, hay, sawdust, or grass found in grease wool.

Virgin or new wool. The term used by the U.S. Federal Trade Commission for wool that has never been used, reclaimed, reworked, reprocessed, or reused from any spun, woven, knitted, felted, manufactured, or used product.

Wasty wool. Grease wool that is short, weak, or tangled and contains large amounts of dirt or sand.

Wholesaling. Selling a product at a discount to a retailer, who will in turn sell it to the customer.

Wool. A term defined by the U.S. Wool Products Labelling Act as the fiber from the fleece of the sheep or lamb or the hair of the Angora or Cashmere goats (and may include the specialty animal fibers from the hair of the camel, alpaca, llama, and vicuna), which has never been reclaimed from any woven or felted wool product. See also *Virgin wool, Reprocessed wool, and Reused wool.*

Yield. The amount of clean wool that can be derived from grease wool in the scouring and carbonizing process.

Yolk. The combination of sweat and a waxy secretion of the sheep's sebaceous glands. More abundant in finer wools, yolk prevents dryness in the wool while on the sheep, produces the off-white color of white wool that has not been bleached, and causes excessive yellowing of fleeces that are shorn after the onset of hot weather.

Sources

Books

If the book you want is not available at a local book or craft shop and no specific source is listed here, you can almost certainly get it from The Unicorn, 1304 Scott Street, Petaluma, CA 94952-1191. They charge a postage rate of $2.50 for one book, plus $.50 for each additional book. Books and periodicals are legitimate business expenses.

Cookbooks Featuring Lamb

The Black Sheep Newsletter Lamb Cookbook (Black Sheep Newsletter, Route 1, Box 288, Scappoose, OR 97056)
Free pamphlets on lamb cookery, from The American Sheep Industry Association (6911 S. Yosemite St., Englewood, CO 80112-1414)

Dyeing

California Dye Plants, by Marilyn Wilkins (Old Orchard Woolens, P.O. Box 932, Weaverville, CA 96093)
The Dye Pot, by Mary Francis Davidson (Unicorn Books, 1304 Scott St., Petaluma, CA 94952-1191)
Hands-On Dyeing, by Blumenthal and Kreider (Interweave Press, 201 E. Fourth St., Loveland, CO 80537)
I'd Rather Dye Laughing, by Jean M. Neal (Unicorn Books, 1304 Scott St., Petaluma, CA 94952-1191)
The New Dyer, by Vinroot and Crowder (Interweave Press, 201 E. Fourth St., Loveland, CO 80537)
North American Dye Plants, by Ann Bliss (Juniper House, P.O. Box 2094, Boulder, CO 80306)
Weeds: A Guide for Dyers, by Ann Bliss (Juniper House, P.O. Box 2094, Boulder, CO 80306)

Feltmaking

Felt Craft, by Sue Freeman (Unicorn Books, 1304 Scott St., Petaluma, CA 94952-1191)

The Felting Book (a booklet from Louet Sales Co., R.R. 4, Prescott, Ontario, Canada K0E 1T0)

Felting by Hand, by Sue Freeman (Unicorn Books, 1304 Scott St., Petaluma, CA 94952-1191)

Feltmaking, by Beverly Gordon

Business Information

Handspinner's Guide to Selling, by Paula Simmons (The Unicorn, 1304 Scott St., Petaluma, CA 94952-1191)

The Law (in Plain English) for Craftspeople, by Leonard DuBoff; edited by Michael Scort (Madrona Publishers, P.O. Box 22667, Seattle, WA 98122)

Locker Hooking

Australian Locker Hooking, by Signe Nickerson (The Crafty Ewe, Box 33, Stevensville, MT 59870)

Loom Building

Handloom Construction, by Joan Koster

Loom Plans (a booklet from The Unicorn, 1304 Scott St., Petaluma, CA 94952-1191)

Sheepraising

The Black Sheep Newsletter Companion, articles from the first five years of *The Black Sheep Newsletter* (Route 1, Box 288, Scappoose, OR 97056)

Breeds of Sheep, by Marilyn Jones (Jones Sheep Farm, Route 2, Box 185, Peabody, KS 66866)

Raising Sheep the Modern Way, by Paula Simmons (Storey Communications, Schoolhouse Rd., Pownal, VT 05261)

Sheep and Wool Science, by M.E. Esminger

The Sheep Book, by Ron Parker

Tanning

The Black Sheep Newsletter, directions for tanning included in an article in the Spring 1984 issue (Route 1, Box 288, Scappoose, OR 97056)

Home Tanning Methods, Leaflet #21005, by G.M. Spurlock (Co-Op Extension Service, University of California, Davis, CA 95616; 34-page pamphlet, free)

Spinning

The Art and Technique of Handspinning, by Allen Fannin (technical writing about spinning)

Hands-On Spinning, by Lee Raven (Interweave Press, 201 E. Fourth St., Loveland, CO 80537)

Handspinner's Guide to Selling, by Paula Simmons

Spinning and Weaving with Wool, by Paula Simmons (Unicorn Books, 1304 Scott St., Petaluma, CA 94952-1191)

Spinning Designer Yarns, by Diane Varney (Interweave Press, 201 East Fourth St., Loveland, CO 80537)

Spinning for Softness and Speed, by Paula Simmons

Spinning Wheel Primer, by Alden Amos (Unicorn Books, 1304 Scott St., Petaluma, CA 94952-1191)

Weaving

Hands-On Weaving, by Barbara Liebler (Interweave Press, 201 East Fourth St., Loveland, CO 80537)

Inkle Weaving, by Helene Bress (The Unicorn, 1304 Scott St., Petaluma, CA 94952-1191)

The Key to Weaving, by Mary Black (a classic)

Spinning and Weaving with Wool, by Paula Simmons (The chapters of this book that are devoted to weaving treat the weaving of handspun yarn, with special techniques.)

The Weaver's Book, by Harriet Tidball (a classic)

Periodicals

Spinning, Weaving and Fiber Arts

These publications would be good places to put classified ads for your products or services. To place ads in "Crafts Available" or "Marketplace" in *The Crafts Report,* write to 87 Wall Street, 2nd Floor, Seattle, WA 98121.

The Craft Report
P.O. Box 1992
Wilmington, DE 19899
(A business newsletter)

Fiberarts
50 College St.
Asheville, NC 28801

Handwoven
201 E. Fourth St.
Loveland, CO 80537

Heddle
Box 1906
Bracebridge, Ontario
PIL 1V8 Canada

The Looming Arts
Box 233
Sedona, AZ 86336

Professional Quilter
Box 4096
St. Paul, MN 55104

Shuttle, Spindle, & Dyepot
120 Mountain Ave., B101
Bloomfield, CT 06002

SpinOff
201 E. Fourth St.
Loveland, CO 80537

Warp and Weft
533 North Adams St.
McMinnville, OR 97128

Sheepraising Periodicals

These are good places to put classified ads for your services or products. Like books, periodicals are usually tax deductible.

Angora Quarterly
P.O. Box 38
Karlin, MI 49647

Sheep!! Magazine
W. 2997 Market St.
Helenville, WI 53137
(the best)

The Shepherd
5696 Johnson
New Washington, OH
44854

The Black Sheep
Newsletter
Route 1, Box 288
Scappoose, OR 97056

Sheep Breeder and
Sheepman
P.O. Box 796
Columbia, MO 65205

Sheep Producer, Farm
Flock & Ranch Journal
Route 2, Box 131A
Arlington, KY 42021

National Wool Grower
8 E. 300 St., Suite 415
Salt Lake City, UT 84111

Sheep Canada
Box 777
Airdrie, Alberta
T0M 0B0 Canada

The Southeastern
Sheepman
277 Main St.
Loganville, GA 30249

Shops Seeking Merchandise such as Weaving, Yarn, Handspun, and Knitted and Woven Garments

The Craft Report
P.O. Box 1992
Wilmington, DE 19899

Every issue contains a listing of shops seeking merchandise, with details of what kind and whether for purchase or consignment. Send $2 for a sample copy of The Craft Report.

Sheepraising Supplies

Sheepman Supply Co.
P.O. Box 100
Barboursville, VA 22923
Wide variety of equipment and supplies for sheep. Send $.50 for catalog.

C.H. Dana Co.
Hyde Park, VT 05655

Nasco Farm and Ranch
901 Janesville Ave.
Ft. Atkinson, WI 53538
or
Nasco West
1524 Princeton Ave.
Modesto, CA 95352

Sheep Coats (Sheepcovers)

Coal Creek Sheep and
Wool
7542 Coal Creek Rd.
Superior, CO 80027

Ewe's Cottage
P.O. Box 183
Roundup, MT 59072

Northfield Meadows
Route 1, Box 110
Dalbo, MN 55017

Powell Sheep Co.
P.O. Box 183
Ramona, CA 92065

Dyes

Cerulean Blue
P.O. Box 5126
Seattle, WA 98105
Send $.50 for catalog

Tinctoria
4318 Stone Way North
Seattle, WA 98103
Send $2 for catalog

W. Cushing and Co.
North St.
Kennebunkport,
ME 04046
Send $1 for color card

Labels

California Dream
2223 El Cajon Blvd.,
No. 209
San Diego, CA 92104
*Fabric labels, including
care and content labels;
free catalog*

Carding & Picking Equipment

Pat Green Carders Ltd.
48793 Chilliwack Lake
Rd.
Sardis, BC V2R 2P1
Canada

Spinning Equipment

Alden Amos
11178 Upper Previtali Rd.
Jackson, CA 95642
*Wool combs, spinning
wheels, spindles, spinning
jenny, charkas; send SASE
for prices*

Glimåkra Looms 'n Yarns
1304 Scott St.
Petaluma, CA
94952-1181

Robert Lee
24451 S. Central Point
Rd.
Canby, OR 97013
*WooLee Winder, auto-
matic flyer and bobbin for
Louet and other spinning
wheels; SASE*

Louet Sales Co.
R.R. 4
Prescott, Ontario
K0E 1T0
Canada
Spinning wheels

Weaving Equipment

Many other suppliers are
mentioned in each issue
of spinning and weaving
publications.

AVL Looms
601 Orange St.
Chico, CA 95928
*Compu-dobby looms; $2
catalog*

Glimåkra Looms 'n Yarn
1304 Scott St.
Petaluma, CA 94952-1181

Robin and Russ
Handweavers
533 North Adams St.
McMinnville, OR 97128

Schacht Spindle
Company
P.O. Box 2157
Boulder, CO 80306

Woolhouse
Box 315
Armstrong, BC V0G 1B0
Canada

Yarn Blockers, Blocking Reels

La Borde Woods
1200 RBC 63
Meeker, CO 81641

Louet Sales Co.
R.R. 4
Prescott, Ontario
K0E 1T0
Canada
Write for list of dealers

Canadian Suppliers

*(selling to the whole North
American continent)*

Canadian Cooperative
Wool Growers
918 First Ave. S.
Lethbridge, Alberta
T1J 0A9
Canada
Sheep supplies and wool

Handcraft Wools
P.O. Box 458
Minden, Ontario
K0M 2K0
Canada
*Spinning and weaving
supplies*

Treenway Crafts
725 Caledonia
Victoria, BC V8T 1E4
Canada
*Spinning and weaving
supplies*

Louet Sales Co.
R.R. 4
Prescott, Ontario
K0E 1T0
Canada
Equipment

Pat Green Carders Ltd.
48793 Chilliwack Lake
Rd.
Sardis, BC V2R 2P1
Canada
*Carders and pickers; free
brochure*

Tanning Supplies

Bucks County Fur
   Products
P.O. Box 204
220½ N. Ambler St.
Quakertown, PA 18951
*Known for high-
quality, low-priced
tanning. Send SASE
for prices and
instructions.*

Eugene Brown
128 Green Ave.
Hempstead NY 11550
*Glutaraldehyde for
tanning. Send SASE
for prices.*

L & M Fur and Woolen
   Enterprises Inc.
103 Erie Ave.
Quakertown, PA 18951
*Custom tanning. Send
SASE for information.*

Rittel's Tanning
   Supplies
107 Dean St.
Taunton, MA 02780
*Tanning Supplies.
Catalog: $.50*

Theo Stern Tanning
   Co.
334 Broadway, Box 55
Sheboygan Falls, WI
   53085
*Send SASE for
information*

Van Dyke's Supply Co.
Box 278
Woonsocket, SD
   57385
*Tannium powder and
other tanning supplies.
Send SASE for prices.*

Labels

Alpha Impressions Inc.
4161 South Main St.
Los Angeles, CA
   90037-2297
*Custom-made woven
and printed labels and
hangtags*

Charm Woven Labels
Box 30027
Portland, OR 97230

Sterling Name Tape
   Co.
Dept. 2053, P.O. Box
   1056
Winsted, CT 06098
Custom labels

♦ *Index* ♦

A

Abbott, Deborah Ann, 104
Advertising, 66, 125-128
Alice in Wonderland, 152-153
Alum, 78
American Textile Manufacturers, 68
Angora goat, 171-172
Australia. *See* Wool, imported

B

Back-to-the-land movement, 4
Batt, 88-89, 95, 101, 114-115, 169
The Black Sheep Newsletter, 22, 42, 170
Blood system, 12-13
Blosser-Rainey, Priscilla, 159-160
Booroola Merino, 15
Border Leicester, 19, 33
Breeding, 5-22, 170-171
    and geographic location, 14
    prolificacy, 11
    sheep types, 10-11
    for specific yarns, 20-21
Breeding stock, 41-43

C

Carbonizing, 59
Carder, 51, 136-138
Carding-and-spinning oil, 92
Carding process, 86-102, 167-168
Catalog, 128
Centrifugal extractor, 143-144
Cerro Mojino Woolworks, 153
Chemical dye, 77, 98
Cheviot, 16, 20, 21
Clun Forest, 17
Cochineal, 78
Columbia, 17
Consignment, 127
Coopworth, 20, 21
Corriedale, 13, 17, 21

Cotswold, 19
Cottage industry
    vs. commercial, 10, 54-55
    entrepreneurs, 152-164
    financial considerations, 51-52, 101, 103-104, 120-121, 123-124
    in remote areas, 165
    with sheep, 23-46
    without sheep, 47-55, 166
Cottage Industry carder, 95, 96, 115, 137-139, 166
Count system, 12-13
Coyote, 29
Craft Report, 126-127
Craft shows, 129-131
Crimp, 12
Crossbreeding, 8, 9-10, 170. *See also* Breeding vs. pure breeding, 8
Custom Colors, 154-155

D

Debouillet, 15
Delaine Merino, 15
Direct selling, 129
Dogs, 27-29
Dorset, 13, 16
Drum carder, 136
Drying process, 74-75, 80-85, 143-144
    rack, 80-85, 144
Dyeing, 54, 77-78, 98, 168

E

Equipment, 51, 135-151
Ethnic market, 45
Ewe, 169-170
    open-faced vs. woolly-faced, 12
    pregnancy, 23-24

F

Facilities, 26-27, 87-88, 121-122
Fairs, selling at, 106, 129-131

Feeding. *See* Sheep, diet
Felt, 71, 116-119, 144, 167-168
Fencing, 27-29
Fiber, 12
   blends, 99-100
   dark, 35, 76-77
   exotic, 165
   hairy, 34-35
Fielding, Kay and Joe, 136, 154-155
Finances. *See* Cottage industry;
   Record keeping
Finnsheep, 11, 17
Fleece. *See also* Wool
   black, 21-22
   defects, 34-37, 89-90
   knitting from, 108-109
   sorting, 63-65, 75-77, 166-167
   skirting, 39-41, 71
Floor looms, 147-148
Flushing, 24
Futons, 115-116

G
Gelenter, Luisa, 158-159
Glimakra Looms 'n Yarns, 148
Gminder, Gisela, 132, 162
Grade (breeding), 170
Grazing, 3-4
Green, Patrick, 136, 137, 141
Green Mountain Spinnery, 155-156
Guard dog, 27-29
Guide to Successful Tapestry Weaving
   (Harvey), 110

H
Hairy fiber, 34-35
Hampshire, 16
Handspinner's Guide to Selling, 127
Handwoven, 128
Harvey, Nancy, 110
Heterosis, 9-10
HGA Educational Directory, 128
Hilltop Wools, 156-157
Home studio shop, 131-133
Hormones, 23

I
Incentive payments, 123-124
Indian Springs Farm, 157

Indigo, 78
Inkle loom, 146
Insurance, 122

J
Jones, Gary, 157-158
Jones, Marilyn, 157-158
Jones Sheep Farm, 157-158
Jumbo Exotic carder, 136
Jumbus Exotica, 100

K
Karakul, 20, 116-117
Kemp, 12, 35
Knitting, 107-108
Knutson, Linda, 77

L
La Lana Wools, 158-159
Lamb chops, 23, 170
Leicester, 19, 21, 171
LeMar, Christine, 153-154
Lessons, giving, 133-134, 169
Lewman, Judy, 57, 160-161
Lincoln, 19, 21, 171
Locker-hooking, 109
Locker lamb, 7, 43-46, 132
Logo, 124-125
Looms, 146-148
Louet carder board, 142-143
Louet Sales Company, 147
Louet spinning wheels, 148-151
Low, Nancy, 163-164

M
Marketing, 53-54, 65-68, 86-87
Mattress covers, 114-115
McCaul, Avalene, 54, 157
McCaul, Jim, 157
Meat, 10, 11, 15-17, 43-46, 169
Menz, Deb, 155
Merian, Lisa Ann, 160
Merino, 12-13, 15, 20, 21, 33, 90, 136,
   171, 172
Micron system, 12-13
Mills, Libbie, 155-156
Mohair goat, 33
Montadale, 17

Montgomery, Charlie, 161-162
Montgomery, Melda, 161-162
Mordant, 77-78
Moths, 101
Mulesing, 172
Munroe, John, 159
Munroe, Marjorie, 159
Munroe Wool Company, 159

N
National Wool Act, 123
Neps, 91-92
New Zealand. *See* Wool, imported
Nutrition. *See* Sheep, diet

O
Oregon Lamb recipe, 46
Oxford, 16

P
Packaging, 68
Pahl, Greg, 163-164
Panama, 17
Parasites, 33-34
Pelts, 111-113
Pendleton Shop, 147
Perendale, 19-20, 20, 21
Picking wool, 92, 139-143
Poisonous plants, 172
Pricing, 89, 124, 165
Public relations, 134
Purebred, 170

Q
Quality control, 92-94. *See also*
    Fleece, defects
Quilt batts, 88-89, 95, 101, 114-115,
    169

R
Rainey, Jerry, 159-160
Ram, 26, 170
Rambouillet, 13, 15, 90, 136, 171
Recipe
    Oregon Lamb, 46
Record keeping
    finances, 122-123
    selling breeding stock, 42

for sheep, 9
Retail selling, 78-79, 129
Ritchie, David, 155-156
River Farm, 159-160
Rolling, 39-41
Romney, 18, 20, 21, 22, 171
Rotenone, 33, 172
Roving, 88, 96-98, 137

S
Saddle pads, 113
Safety, 102, 122, 140-141
Schacht Spindle Company, 146-147,
    147-148
Scrub, 170
Shearing, 37-39, 59-61, 65, 66, 67
Sheep, 169-172
    black, 21-22, 170
    breeding, 5-22, 170-171
    breeding stock, 41-43
    buying, 169-170
    diet, 3-4, 24-26
    fine-wool breeds, 14-15
    and grazing, 3-4
    hoof, 6, 26
    jaw, 6
    long-wool breeds, 18-20
    management, 23-46
    meat breeds, 15-17
    medium-wool breeds, 17-18
    nose, 6
    shelter, 26-27
    teeth, 8, 170, 171
    udder, 6, 8
    worms, 26
Sheepcover, 29-33
    patterns, 32
Sheepdog, 27-29
Sheepraising and wool processing,
    1-2
Shelter, 171-172
Shropshire, 16
Shuttle, Spindle and Dyepot, 128
Simmons, Paula, 110, 138, 140
Sitzman, Sandy, 163
Skirting, 39-41, 61, 71
Sorting process, 75-77, 80-85, 166-167
Southdown, 16, 20, 21
Spinner's Hill, 160

Spinning, 1, 2, 4, 11, 65, 88-89, 168, 170, 171
  guilds, 67
  wheels, 148-151
Spinning and Weaving with Wool, 146
SpinOff, 128
Spring Creek Farm, 160-161
Springwater Spinoffs, 161
Storage, 61-62, 101-102, 166-167
Stough, Alice, 108, 152-153
Stringy yolk, 35
Suffolk, 16, 170
Sullivan, Kathleen, 161
Synthetic Dyes for Natural Fibers (Knutson), 77

T
Table loom, 147
Table-top drum carder, 95, 136
Table-top rover, 137
Tanning, 45, 111-114
Tapestry, 110
Tapestry loom, 147
Targhee, 17
Taylor, Connie, 153
Taylor, Sam, 153
Teeth, 8, 170, 171
Ticks, 6, 33, 172
Tunis, 17
Twins, 7, 11, 24
Tying, 40-41

U
Udder, 6, 8

V
Van Stralen, Jan, 156-157
Van Stralen, Trudy, 156-157
Vegetable dye, 77-78, 98

W
Walker, Linda Berry, 18
Wall Street Journal, 69, 114
Washing process, 71-75, 92, 168

Weaving, 2, 4, 109-111
Wholesale selling, 66-67, 79-80, 126-127
Wilson, Claire, 155-156
Woodland Woolworks, 161-162
Wool. *See also* Fleece
  blending, 98-100
  buying vs. raising, 48-50, 166
  characteristics of, 3
  cotted, 36-37, 90
  dark fibers, 35, 76-77
  factory preferences, 68-69
  fleece defects, 34-37, 89-90
  imported, 56-58
  quality, 58-59
  raw, 56-69
  reselling, 50-51
  short, 90
  stained, 37, 90
  steely, 36, 90
  tender, 36, 89
  tippy, 89
  value of, 1
  washed, 70-85
  weathered, 37
Wool and Feathers, 162
Wool and wood businesses, 103
Woolee winder, 151
Woolgatherings, 163
Wool processing. *See also* specific processes such as Washing process
  effects of, 91
  grading, 12-13, 62-65, 167
  picking wool, 92, 94-95, 139-143
  without sheep, 2-3, 47-55
  and sheepraising, 1-2
  teasing wool, 92
  vegetation in wool, 59, 92
Wool sources, 52-53
Wooly Hill Farm, 163-164
Worms, 34

Y
Yarn, 1, 20-21, 65-66, 104-107, 144-146
  blocker, 144-146